Incarceration and human rights

MANCHESTER
1824

Manchester University Press

The Oxford Amnesty Lectures

Also available
'War on terror': The Oxford Amnesty Lectures 2006 *ed. Chris Miller*

Incarceration and human rights

The Oxford Amnesty Lectures 2007

edited by

Melissa McCarthy

Manchester University Press

Manchester and New York

distributed in the United States exclusively by Palgrave Macmillan

While copyright in the volume as a whole is vested in Manchester University Press, copyright in individual chapters belongs to Oxford Amnesty Lectures, and no chapter may be reproduced wholly or in part without the express permission in writing of both Oxford Amnesty Lectures and publisher.

Published by Manchester University Press
Oxford Road, Manchester M13 9NR, UK
and Room 400, 175 Fifth Avenue, New York, NY 10010, USA
www.manchesteruniversitypress.co.uk

Distributed in the United States exclusively by
Palgrave Macmillan, 175 Fifth Avenue, New York,
NY 10010, USA

Distributed in Canada exclusively by
UBC Press, University of British Columbia, 2029 West Mall,
Vancouver, BC, Canada V6T 1Z2

British Library Cataloguing-in-Publication Data
A catalogue record for this book is available from the British Library

Library of Congress Cataloging-in-Publication Data applied for

ISBN 978 07190 8180 4 hardback
ISBN 978 07190 8181 1 paperback

First published 2010

The publisher has no responsibility for the persistence or accuracy of URLs for any external or third-party internet websites referred to in this book, and does not guarantee that any content on such websites is, or will remain, accurate or appropriate.

Typeset in 10.5/12.5pt GraphArnoPro by Graphicraft Limited, Hong Kong
Printed in Great Britain by CPI Antony Rowe Ltd, Chippenham

Contents

Preface

The Oxford Amnesty Lectures is a registered charity. Its purpose is to raise funds for Amnesty International and to raise awareness of human rights in the academic and wider communities. It is otherwise independent of Amnesty International. It began as a fund-raising project for the Oxford Amnesty group and is now one of the world's leading lecture series. To date, Oxford Amnesty Lectures has raised over £108,000 for Amnesty International.

Foreword

The Oxford Amnesty Lectures 2007 took place in January, February and March. The speakers in the series were Lawrence Gostin, Loïc Wacquant, Anne Owers, Shami Chakrabarti and Jack Mapanje; and, though not included in this volume, Roger Graef, Robert Badinter and Linda Colley. I am grateful to all these, and to Thomas Mathiesen, who was unable to speak in person but who has contributed a chapter. Where a lecture has been reworked or written at a later date, I have noted the final date in an endnote.

I am also grateful to those who acted as introducers at the lectures and who have responded to these texts: Roger Hood, Stephen Shute, Ian Loader, Liora Lazarus, Alexis Tadié, Roger Zetter, William Beinart, David Downes and Jonny Steinberg. Their efficiency and willingness to contribute are greatly appreciated.

Thanks to Bloodaxe Books for permission to include two poems by Jack Mapanje in Chapter 6.

Many thanks are due to the other members of the Oxford Amnesty Lectures organising committee, without whom the series and publication would never have come to pass. In 2007, these were Cathryn Costello, Liora Lazarus, Chris Miller, Nick Owen, Fabienne Pagnier, Deana Rankin, Richard Scholar, Kate Tunstall, Katrin Wehling and Wes Williams. I extend particular thanks to OAL co-founder Chris Miller for his tireless help in refining lines of thought.

Melissa McCarthy

Notes on contributors

SHAMI CHAKRABARTI has been Director of the British human rights organisation Liberty since 2003. Previously a barrister, she worked in the Home Office for Conservative and Labour governments on counter-terror, asylum and criminal justice. As Liberty's Director, she speaks and broadcasts widely on the importance to democratic society of the post-war human rights framework. She is a governor of the London School of Economics.

DAVID DOWNES is Professor Emeritus of Social Administration at the London School of Economics. He was editor of the *British Journal of Criminology* from 1985 to 1990, and is an editor of the Clarendon Studies in Criminology series for the Oxford University Press. His current work looks at mass imprisonment, comparative trends in crime, inequality, the regulation of drug use, welfare and criminal justice.

LAWRENCE O. GOSTIN is an international expert on law and public health. Among multiple academic and professional distinctions he is Professor of Global Health Law at Georgetown University, and Professor of Public Health at the Johns Hopkins University. He has served on Federal Advisory Committees on HIV/AIDS, and was Legal Director of MIND (the National Association for Mental Health, in Britain) from 1975 to 1982.

LIORA LAZARUS is Fellow and Tutor in Law at St Anne's College, Oxford, following research at the University of Cape Town, the London School of Economics and the Max Planck Institute. Her research interests are in comparative human rights and criminal justice. She is co-editor, with B. Goold, of *Security and Human Rights* (Oxford: Hart, 2007), and author of *Contrasting Prisoners' Rights* (Oxford: Oxford University Press, 2004).

IAN LOADER is Professor of Criminology and Director of the Centre for Criminology at Oxford University. His latest book, written with Neil Walker, is *Civilizing Security* (Cambridge: Cambridge University Press, 2007). He has written widely on contemporary transformations in policing and security, and on the intersections between politics, criminology and crime control. He is a member of the Commission on English Prisons Today.

JACK MAPANJE, a poet, linguist and editor, is Senior Lecturer in Creative Writing at Newcastle University. For his academic achievement, contribution to poetry and human rights, he received the 1988 Rotterdam Poetry International Award and the 2002 African Literature Association (USA) Fonlon-Nichols Award. His fifth and latest book of poems, *Beasts of Nalunga* (Tarset, Northumberland: Bloodaxe Books, 2007), was shortlisted for the UK's Forward Prize for Poetry.

THOMAS MATHIESEN is Professor Emeritus of Sociology of Law at Oslo University, the culmination of a distinguished academic career. In 1978 he received the Denis Carroll prize at the World Congress of the International Criminological Society, for the book *The Politics of Abolition* (London: Martin Robertson and Oslo: Universitetsforlaget, 1974). He was a founder of KROM, the Norwegian Association for Penal Reform, in 1968, and served as its first chair, until 1973.

ANNE OWERS has been Her Majesty's Chief Inspector of Prisons since 2001. She was previously director of the law reform and human rights organisation JUSTICE for nine years, where she helped to secure the setting up of the Criminal Cases Review Commission. She has served on various government committees including the Home Office Task Force on the implementation of the Human Rights Act.

STEPHEN SHUTE is Professor of Criminal Law and Criminal Justice and Head of the School of Law, Politics and Sociology at the University of Sussex. His work on high-risk offenders, parole and sentencing has influenced judicial practice in the UK and internationally. Formerly a professor and Deputy Pro-Vice-Chancellor at the University of Birmingham, he serves on the editorial board of, among other journals, *Criminal Law and Philosophy*.

JONNY STEINBERG is a writer, journalist and policy analyst. Two of his books about life in South Africa during transition – *Midlands* (Johannesburg: Jonathan Ball, 2002) and *The Number* (Johannesburg: Jonathan Ball, 2004) – have won the Alan Paton Prize for non-fiction. Following work at Johannesburg's Centre for the Study of Violence and Reconciliation, and a Rhodes scholarship at Oxford, he holds an Open Society Fellowship.

LOÏC WACQUANT is Professor of Sociology at the University of California, Berkeley, and Researcher at the Centre de sociologie européenne, Paris. His books, translated into a dozen languages, include *Urban Outcasts: A Comparative Sociology of Advanced Marginality* (London: Polity Press, 2008), and *Punishing the Poor: The Neoliberal Government of Social Insecurity* (Durham and London: Duke University Press, 2009).

ROGER ZETTER is Professor of Refugee Studies and Director of the Refugee Studies Centre at Oxford University, where from 1988 to 2001 he was Founding Editor of the *Journal of Refugee Studies*. He advises governmental, non-governmental and intergovernmental agencies on many aspects of refugee and humanitarian assistance. Following research into Mozambican, Greek-Cypriot and Great Lakes refugees, he now focuses on Europe and the UK.

MELISSA MCCARTHY is a writer and arts curator who works from Durban and London.

Introduction

Oxford Amnesty Lectures (OAL) has as its first *raison d'etre* the raising of funds for Amnesty International. It does so through an annual series of lectures which consider human rights in light of a particular theme. In 2007 the theme was incarceration, an apposite topic when one remembers Amnesty International's founding narrative, that of Peter Benenson reading about two Portuguese students being imprisoned. The result was international mobilisation, political pressure, and the talking out loud about first two, then thousands, of people who could otherwise have remained incarcerated and silenced. This 'talking out loud' is OAL's second remit: to promote debate. In this book we do so through the contributions of twelve thoughtful experts, whose words are informed by personal experience in prisons (and asylums and detention centres), by professional engagement with policy and practice, and by academic knowledge of law, history, sociology, criminology and literature.

In Part I, 'Behind bars', Anne Owers, Shami Chakrabarti and Lawrence O. Gostin take us inside places of detainment, looking at the treatment of various groups.

As Her Majesty's Inspector of Prisons, Owers is responsible for inspecting and reporting on all those held in prisons and some other facilities in England, Wales and Northern Ireland, but, as she says, her work is influential beyond these borders. She describes the work of her Inspectorate, and makes the important point that her reports are based on absolute standards, judging 'against what is right, rather than what is necessarily immediately achievable'. She raises particular concerns about the treatment of minorities, including women, ethnic minorities, children and asylum seekers; and draws attention to the sad fact that, in prison, those with mental illness and substance abuse problems form, rather, a majority. Underpinning her judgements are the human rights based tests that determine a 'healthy prison': safety, dignity, purposeful activity and resettlement.

Gostin, too, sets out four rights – liberty, dignity, equality and entitlement – that he seeks for his particular demographic, those with mental illness, and he details how international law has changed, slowly and incrementally, to provide better support for these rights. Despite this progress, he also traces a grim history of deinstitutionalisation, with asylums closing only for their residents to be cared for, not 'in the community', but on the streets and back behind the bars of prisons. With a background in academia and policy advocacy, his main focus is on the USA and the European Community, but he also describes progress in the Americas and at the global scale of the United Nations and the World Health Organization, and he raises the question of the 'cultural acceptance' of mental illness, which leads to differing national practices of detainment.

Chakrabarti, Director of British human rights organisation Liberty, considers the case of asylum seekers held in detention in the United Kingdom. She too places this within the international context of rights legislation, particularly the 1951 *Convention Relating to the Status of Refugees*,[1] and within a history of Britain and 'fortress Europe' since the Second World War. She raises the puzzle of the 'inter-dependent world', in which military intervention or aid (or, though she does not mention it, capital) might move freely, but people find it harder to cross borders. And when they do manage to arrive at a potential place of safety, how their treatment breaks faith with previous promises. The movement of people is a theme addressed in earlier Oxford Amnesty Lectures,[2] but Chakrabarti sets out how it's still a pressing matter, and how the refugee is 'at the heart of modern notions of human rights'.

These texts all derive from lectures given by the contributors to a live, and lively, audience in Oxford, who have an opportunity for question and answer after each lecture. OAL gives a flavour of this sense of dialogue by asking a respondent to discuss, dispute or otherwise engage with each lecture text.

Liora Lazarus does so by combining praise of Owers' practice with a troubled analysis of rights theory in the current climate, looking in particular at the ideas of 'public protection' and 'security'. Honing in on a comment that the prevention of reoffending is a key element in the 'core human right' of public protection, Lazarus takes issue with this instrumental view, as she does with a growing 'culture of control', which is sceptical of rights and fuelled by political rhetoric. She moots, instead, a 'right to insecurity' – an unavoidable adjunct to freedom, and 'a necessary concomitant of the liberal society'.

Roger Zetter takes Chakrabarti's account of the detention of refugees and expands from it a dissection of 'diminishing rights' in Britain. He identifies a polarisation between 'insiders', with their shaky sense of 'national identity', and the feared 'other' – the migrant, refugee or perceived potential terrorist. But it is not only the rights and treatment of the incomer that are at stake, as restrictions that start out reserved for groups perceived as threatening quickly spread to the population as a whole, infringing everyone's individual liberties and freedom of speech. Rights and responsibilities are often paired in populist discourse, but Zetter casts them in a different light, when he follows the rights lost in a 'persecutory' environment with the moral obligations that we in a liberal democracy are failing to discharge.

Stephen Shute amplifies Gostin's account of deinstitutionalisation by offering a survey of what the rules are that govern the treatment of prisoners in England and Wales. He shows how case law, legislation and international instruments shape this treatment, his account covering not just the core human rights of life and liberty, but also some 'secondary rights' in the economic, cultural and social sphere. He closes with a discussion of the right to vote, over which the UK Government is in conflict with the European Court of Human Rights.

The chapters in Part I might paint a gloomy picture of conditions in prisons, but they also show that improvements can be made, and that there is pressure for both better standards and treatment, and adherence to the absolute standards which exist, underpinned by human rights instruments. The main ones referred to by the contributors include, on the United Nations front, the Geneva or Refugee Convention as mentioned above, which entered into force in 1954; the *Optional Protocol to the Convention against Torture and other Cruel, Inhuman or Degrading Treatment or Punishment* (Opcat), which came into effect in 2006; the *International Covenant on Civil and Political Rights*, which entered into force in 1976 and which states as Article 10, 'All persons deprived of their liberty shall be treated with humanity and with respect for the inherent dignity of the human person'; and, of course, the *Universal Declaration of Human Rights* of 1948, especially Article 3: 'Everyone has the right to life, liberty and security of person.' Owers and Chakrabarti also refer to the *Convention on the Rights of the Child*, which entered into force in 1990.[3]

At the European level, the most commonly mentioned instrument is the *European Convention on Human Rights and Fundamental Freedoms* of 1950, known as the European Convention.[4] Within it, of particular relevance to incarceration are Article 5, the right to liberty and security of person; Article 3, prohibiting torture; and Articles 6, the right to fair trial and 7, the prohibition of punishment without law.

These are the human rights instruments that currently govern incarceration. In 'Behind bars', the contributors examine what might be done better within something like existing structures – structures both physical and organisational. As Owers points out, her remit is specifically to inspect and report on what is done in prisons, 'not to validate the decision to detain'. But neither she nor the other contributors ignore the broader context, of the historical, political and social networks within which prisons function. There seems to be broad alignment in all these texts with Owers' description of prisons as 'a microcosm of what is going wrong with the rest of society', and an agreement with her dictum that better resources are urgently needed outside prisons, as well as inside.

In Part II, 'Beyond the prison', the contributors are less immediately concerned with the specifics of what happens behind bars. Building, in particular, on Zetter and Lazarus's lead, they set out a reconfiguration of how we might theorise, and act, on issues of incarceration and human rights. Loïc Wacquant, a sociologist, Thomas Mathiesen, a professor of sociology of law and an activist, and Jack Mapanje, a poet, are all well-versed in the problems, experiences and practice of prisons, but their essays take a broader standpoint.

Guided by the thinking of his former teacher and colleague Pierre Bourdieu, Wacquant places the prison within an ever-strengthening field of neoliberal social control, in which the insecurity of a deregulated, post-Keynsian economy is used to perpetuate a separate space for the outcast and marginalised. He states that a proper understanding of this 'punitive turn' requires combining a materialist analysis of economic relations with an appreciation of the symbolic power that prisons communicate. Looking first at the USA and then at the Western European countries that follow its 'politics of poverty', Wacquant describes the penal system and the workfare state (no longer welfare) as intermeshed, both of them working to control and tame populations – women, ethnic minorities, immigrants – that had threatened disruption.

Ian Loader responds to Wacquant by seeing whether, despite the grip of neoliberal penality, there might be routes out of this morass. One grappling hook for dealing with the issue, for Loader, is the clarity with which Wacquant identifies and rejects ideas about prisons that are commonsensical but wrong. Loader's own suggestion for progress also looks to economics, but does so in the context of the 2009 'credit crunch', hoping that, as there are calls for financial excess to be replaced by the burnt fingers of caution, so too in place of the damage of hyperpenality, we might move to 'penal moderation'.

Mathiesen brings his characteristically humane mindset to bear on the issues. In his ten-pronged argument for a moratorium on prison-building, he sets out the ostensible rationales for prisons in order to refute them, with examples from his extensive work as an academic and activist. Mathiesen paints a broad landscape in which prisons are just one link in the chain of control that stretches from long before crime to long after; from police surveillance and the prediction of risk, to prison, parole and after, integrated into one diffuse 'punishment chain'. But he also suggests the possibility for resistance, building on the model of peace movements and protest.

David Downes expands on Mathiesen's arguments, emphasising an important point (also a concern of Wacquant's) about the lack of connection between crime and punishment. As well as seconding the prison moratorium in terms of what is wrong with prisons, Downes describes a 'more constructive and less damaging' response to crime, that of restorative justice. He sets out its benefits and limitations, offering it as a counterbalance to the narrative, often heard from politicians, that 'prison works'.

In his essay, Mapanje offers a personal story of beyond the prison: firstly, of the international support network that helped to obtain his freedom, and then of what happened after his release. Strategies for coping behind bars had to mutate into ways of surviving the freedom of unfriendly exile in a world that had moved on despite his absence. Mapanje's tactic, and his gift, has been to develop a field of study called Literatures of Incarceration, which incorporates work from imprisoned African writers, Latin American exiles and other prisoners, writing from the Holocaust and the gulag, and classic Western works. Perhaps depressing, but imaginative and full of a dark humour, these are artworks that can be enjoyed, can help spread knowledge, and can assist in a reassessing and reimagining of the reader's place in the world.

Jonny Steinberg picks up on the power of narrative by bringing in two stories of imprisonment from South Africa, one about Nelson Mandela, the other a tale from his research into prison gangs and their oral mythology. Responding to Mapanje, he describes incarceration as 'a tool' that Mapanje used, successfully, to carve out a space of survival. Steinberg's language reshapes Mapanje's experience into a concrete object. And it is reshapings – of a painful history into a tool for education; of harmful practices into more constructive ones; of certain understandings of prisons into counter-narratives and transformed conceptions – that all these contributors offer.

Each contribution stands alone, but we might extract certain threads that seem to run through the whole.

Firstly, there is concern about the media, and about a discourse on prisons (and the people in them) which is populist, hysterical and self-fuelling. The hope behind this book is that it might offer an arena for a more considered set of voices. Instead of hard words on prisons, we might heed Mathiesen's call for 'hard thinking'.

A second recurring theme is that of economics. The constant power struggle between classes is central to Wacquant's thesis, while Mathiesen agrees that prison-building is 'an intensification of the war against the poor. Not poverty, but the poor.' Downes discusses the economic impact of US mass imprisonment, and, though Wacquant decries the 'prison-industrial complex' label as oversimplified – 'the wrapping [not] the package' – a work such as Christian Parenti's Lockdown America is a vivid introduction to some of the related ideas.[5] Also relevant to both Wacquant and Mathiesen, and, for different reasons, to Mapanje, is the figure of the scholar Angela Davis. Her work locates prison as a function of the capitalist mode of economy, as a time-based and deeply racialised institution which also traces roots to slavery, the reservation and the internment camp.[6]

In this book, the main places under discussion are the USA, the UK and Western Europe, with detours to Canada, the Americas and southern Africa. The contributors point to diverse practices in different countries, but a third underlying theme is that of the flow and movement of ideas, influences and people.

Mass imprisonment on the US model spreads to, or is resisted in, other places. People migrate, or are moved, their arrival bringing new social configurations and new uses of the prison. Borders and realms of influence change, with imperialist expansion (and reflux) lurking in many of these texts. Chakrabarti discusses the upheavals and aftermath of the Second World War, and mentions that migration is influenced by 'family, linguistic and other cultural ties borne of the imperial past'. Mapanje looks back to colonial rule and forwards to consequences of the invasion of Iraq, reminding us with respect to Guantanamo that 'Although we like to forget the point, for many years such prisons have become an integral part of Western civilisation.'

And in line with these flows, the very idea of prison is by no means fixed; for an account of its variation through time and place, and the fact that it is itself a reaction to other modes of punishment, see, for example, the discussion by Pieter Spierenburg in 'The body and the state: Early Modern Europe'.[7]

The final area of fluidity must be between the two halves of the title, to look at what might emerge from the yoking together of incarceration and human rights. Certainly prisons are places where, with the fundamental right of liberty suspended, human rights can be observed or ignored, promoted or disregarded. The contributors show us how to judge, and improve, prison through the prism of rights. But the connection, they also suggest, works the other way. We should look at rights through the prison: what are the processes by which it upholds or distorts rights; whose rights are threatened, whose values upheld? The problems that prisons raise – practical, theoretical, moral – are problems that we need to engage with in order to refine our ideas about human rights, in order to exercise and fully enjoy those rights.

Notes

1 See note 3.
2 See Kate E. Tunstall (ed.), *Displacement, Asylum, Migration: The Oxford Amnesty Lectures 2004* (Oxford: Oxford University Press, 2006).
3 See www2.ohchr.org/english/law/ for links to the International Bill of Human Rights, and to the core international human rights instruments, both those mentioned above and the *Standard Minimum Rules* and the *Basic Principles for the Treatment of Prisoners* (accessed 28 February 2009).
4 Viewable via www.echr.coe.int/echr/ (accessed 28 February 2009).
5 C. Parenti, *Lockdown America: Police and Prisons in the Age of Crisis* (London: Verso, 1999).
6 Angela Y. Davis, *Are Prisons Obsolete?* (New York: Seven Stories Press, 2003).
7 Pieter Spierenburg, 'The body and the state: Early Modern Europe', in Norval Morris and David J. Rothman (eds), *The Oxford History of the Prison: The Practice of Punishment in Western Society* (Oxford: Oxford University Press, 1997).

Part I
Behind bars

1 Anne Owers

Prisons inspection and the protection of human rights[1]

This essay is about why independent inspection of places of custody is a necessary part of human rights protection, and how that independence is manifested and preserved in practice.

In this society, incarceration is the highest penalty that the state can impose – and, increasingly, that is the case in many countries of the world as international pressure to abolish the death penalty grows. The expansion of the Council of Europe and the insistence that all new member states, when they sign up to the *European Convention on Human Rights*, also accept Protocol 6, which outlaws capital punishment, have hugely extended this area. But it has also thrown into even greater prominence the need to monitor and examine conditions in custody, in states that have limited resources but are now finding themselves holding more prisoners, and for much longer terms.

Within the Council of Europe, the role of the Committee for the Prevention of Torture (CPT) has been crucial. It is independent of states parties and has the power at any time to go into any place of custody in any member state. It reports to the state authorities on the treatment of those detained. Though those reports are not made public, states must make a response – and risk action at the European Court of Human Rights if there are significant breaches of its key articles, particularly the prohibition on torture and inhuman and degrading treatment.

The notion of independent monitoring of places of detention has acquired even more extensive international underpinning. In June 2006, the new *Optional Protocol to the UN Convention against Torture* (Opcat) came into effect, having acquired a sufficient number of signatories – including the United Kingdom, which was one of the first to sign up.[2] It approaches monitoring principally from a domestic, rather than an international, perspective. It requires each state party to have in place an independent 'national preventive mechanism' which can regularly visit and report on all places of detention. The international mechanisms to ensure compliance are more limited than the European ones: there is no court with overarching jurisdiction, and only a committee of experts with few resources, reliant on information from, and the vigilance of, domestic bodies.

The UK was able to sign up to Opcat very swiftly because we already have in place a robust and independent domestic system for inspecting prisons and most other places of custody. The principal mechanism for this is, of course, the Prisons Inspectorate. Set up in its present form in 1981, it now has statutory responsibility for inspecting prisons and young offender institutions (YOIs) in England and Wales and all places of immigration detention within the UK. It acts under the statutory authority of the Chief Inspector of Criminal Justice in Northern Ireland to inspect prisons and YOIs there too. By invitation, it also inspects the Military Corrective Training Centre (the armed services' only central detention centre), and prisons in the Channel Islands and Isle of Man. Moreover, we are currently working with colleagues in the Inspectorate of Constabulary to develop a methodology and mechanism for regular inspection of police custody suites (as we are with Courts Inspectorate colleagues in relation to court cells). Other bodies – the Mental Health Act Commission and Ofsted, respectively – are responsible for inspecting secure mental hospitals, and secure training centres for children. Independent monitoring, on a regular basis, is also carried out by local independent monitoring boards (IMBs), which are groups of volunteer citizens with the right of entry into their local prison. Their continuous presence provides a valuable complementary role to inspection.

We hardly need reminding why international and domestic law places such importance on independent and regular inspection of all places of detention. They operate out of sight, and often out of mind, of the public. They are places where power is with the custodian, not the detainee; and where detainees are dependent on the humanity of their custodians for everything, from small dignities (for example, being able to have a pillow or toothbrush) to freedom from abuse (intimidation or even physical violence). We have seen examples of the latter in our prison system, most acutely in the events at Wormwood Scrubs during the 1990s; and, though it is rare, I have come across examples, particularly in segregation units, where prison managers have not been sufficiently alert to abusive cultures or behaviour.

Abuse, or a lack of humanity, need not be planned or deliberate. Because they operate behind closed doors, prisons and places of detention can develop ways of behaviour that come to be accepted as normal because that is the way things have always been done. All institutions have a default setting of convenience, and it is all too easy for places of detention to reflect the convenience of staff, rather than the needs of detainees. Prisons, too, rightly focus on security: the task of keeping prisoners in, and running prisons safely. But 'security' can all too often be an all-purpose excuse for saying no. A ban on nail clippers at Harmondsworth immigration removal centre was one example of that; another was a prison where prisoners were denied plugs for their sinks (where they often had to wash themselves) in case the chains could be used as weapons. No risk assessment or security analysis had been done in either case: it simply made prison or custody officers feel more comfortable – and more in control.

Protecting the human rights of those detained is obviously central to independent inspection. But there is also a broader human rights perspective. It has been suggested that human rights and public protection are in opposition to one another; and that over-concern with human rights can result in damage to the safety of the public. I would very strongly refute that. Public protection – the ability of people to live in safety, without threats to their life and well-being – is itself a core human right. The state therefore has a positive duty to do all it can to protect the life and human dignity of the public, as well as prison staff and prison officers. That means that prisons must be safe places which contribute actively to public protection, by making it less, rather than more, likely that those incarcerated will reoffend once released.

The Prisons Inspectorate and its work

My Inspectorate has developed four human rights based tests of what we call a 'healthy prison'. First, prisoners, even the most vulnerable, should be held in safety. Second, all prisoners should be treated with respect for their human dignity. Third, they should all be able to engage in purposeful activity, which provides essential skills and training. Finally, they should be prepared for resettlement back into the community. The first two are primarily about the safe and decent treatment of prisoners (and prisons that are unsafe for prisoners are often unsafe for staff too). The second two in addition address the effective protection of the public in the longer term. We have found that these tests, suitably adapted, can be used to assess the health of all custodial environments, wherever they are and for however short a time people are detained there.

In making assessments of how well establishments are performing against those tests, we do not rely on the standards of the inspected organisation: whether that is the public sector Prison Service, a private sector prison run under contract, or an immigration removal centre. We have developed our own criteria, called *Expectations*, which are based on best practice and human rights standards, and which set out in detail what we expect to find in every area of custodial life, from reception to resettlement, from family visits to segregation.[3] We have separate *Expectations* for juveniles (aged under eighteen) and for immigration detainees. This is one important pillar of our independence. It means that we are judging places of detention against what is right, rather than what can be immediately achieved. For example, in our overcrowded prisons, we will often find two men sharing a cell meant for one, with an unscreened toilet where one of them has to sit to eat meals, and where they may spend twenty-three hours a day. The Prison Service does not want to hold people in those conditions, but at present it has no choice. But unless we continue to point out that it is not decent or right, there is a real danger that what has become normal will be accepted as normative.

All our inspection reports are published, in full.[4] And the timing and the content are matters for me alone. There are two other important pillars of our independence. One is the right, at any time and without warning, to go into any place of detention and to have immediate access to all those held there. Inspectors carry their own keys, and are not chaperoned as they go around. They can talk in private to prisoners, detainees and staff, read every document, and observe everything that goes on. Over half of our inspections take place without warning. This is a vital power – not least because, while a small team cannot carry out inspections as often as we would like, each governor in the country knows that tomorrow could be the day when the Inspectorate turns up.

Secondly, we carry out confidential surveys of those being detained, asking them about all aspects of life in custody. We now have an extensive database, so that we can compare one establishment with others of a similar type, or with the responses we got when we last inspected it. Prisoners' views are not always right, but it is noticeable how often prisoners have an accurate picture of their place of detention, its strengths and weaknesses; and if they have a poor perception, it is important for managers to find out why. It is gratifying that the Prison Service, which was initially very opposed to such surveys, now carries out a qualitative exercise with prisoners, called measuring the quality of prison life, as part of each of its own internal standards audits.

Let me address each of our healthy prison tests in turn, with some examples of the things that inspections have found, and that the Inspectorate has tried to change.

Once the state takes someone into custody, it acquires a positive duty of care for their safety. That means trying to ensure that they are safe from others (whether other prisoners or staff) and also that they are safe from themselves (from the risk of self-inflicted death or serious harm). Levels of suicide and self-harm have been high in prisons, reflecting the imported vulnerability of many of those who enter prisons, but also the increased vulnerability that can result from incarceration itself. When I took up the position as Chief Inspector of Prisons in 2001, suicides in prison were running at about two a week; and a disproportionate number were women. It is worth reflecting on the background of many of the women (and men) who end up in prison. It is estimated that between 70 per cent and 80 per cent suffer from some form of mental disorder; and about the same proportions will have substance abuse problems, including hazardous levels of drinking. The two are not unconnected.

Women have other significant problems: around one in ten will have attempted suicide; half say they have experienced domestic violence and a third, sexual assault. They also have a range of factors that mean that prison exacerbates that vulnerability. Two-thirds are mothers, and half are primary carers of children under sixteen. For eight out of ten women this will be their first serious separation from their children; unlike men, only 25 per cent can expect their partner to look after them, and a third will lose their home (and therefore their possessions and probably their children) while in custody. They are much more likely than men to be held at a considerable distance from home, the more so now that women's prisons are being redeployed to hold men because of population pressure.

Suicide prevention has been a major focus of the Inspectorate. In 1999, we published a thematic report, 'Suicide is everyone's concern', which argued for a whole-prison approach to supporting the most vulnerable. Many of the key recommendations in that report have now been implemented. The Prison Service has put in place a more proactive and multi-disciplinary process for supporting potentially vulnerable prisoners. A great deal of effort has also gone into providing support during the crucial early days of custody, when suicides are most likely to happen: partly because of the shock of imprisonment, and partly because a majority of prisoners are withdrawing from addictive drugs. Many prisons have now put in place first night centres, where new prisoners' individual needs can be assessed and support can be given. We inspect them closely – and we are less than impressed by prisons which imagine that putting up a notice saying 'first night centre' is all that is needed, while prisoners are put in filthy cells, without adequate bedding, and with no opportunity for one-to-one discussion with staff or trained prisoners.

Detoxification in prisons has also improved considerably. We no longer find, as we did at Styal in 2002, that women are fitting and vomiting in their cells as they withdraw from drugs. But it needs to be noted that between that inspection and the eventual implementation of proper first night and detoxification procedures at Styal, six women died, all in the early days of custody and all with histories of drug addiction.

The suicide rate in prisons has, thankfully, dropped, despite significant rises in the prison population. In 2006 there were 63 self-inflicted deaths, compared to 104 in 2004; and crucially far fewer of them took place within the first seven days (only 8 per cent, compared to 32 per cent). That is an example of how inspection, allied to the willingness to change of those being inspected, can change things. However, there are a couple of caveats. First, the levels of self-harm, particularly among women, remain high. Women are only 5 per cent of the prison population, but they account for 52 per cent of all incidents of self-harm. Moreover, 31 per cent of those incidents involve young women under twenty-one, who are only 1 per cent of the female population. In one women's prison, there were around six self-harm incidents a day. They could include horrific and repeated acts – like the young woman who not only opened her veins but inserted biros into them. Sometimes prisons have resorted to desperate measures to prevent self-harm escalating into death, such as putting women in strip clothing in unfurnished cells. That does nothing, however, to tackle the underlying causes of self-harm; it merely postpones its occurrence. Interestingly, the women's prisons with the lowest incidence of self-harm are also those with the highest levels of activity, and the best staff–prisoner relationships.

Second, the continuing alarming rise in the prison population makes it all the more difficult to support vulnerable prisoners properly, particularly in the crucial early days. The throughput of prisoners in busy local prisons – sometimes a hundred a day – makes it hard to identify the vulnerable, or indeed those who may be risks to other prisoners when, inevitably, two strangers are locked up in the same cell. More prisoners are held further from home, with long journeys: at one juvenile prison recently, young people had arrived as late as 2.0 a.m., often after a day spent in court cells. And at times of maximum pressure prisoners have spent their first nights not in prisons but in police cells, where there are none of the early support mechanisms that most prisons have now put in place. As an example, on one night we monitored in February 2007 there were nearly four hundred prisoners in police cells; and at least twenty who did not even get that far, but spent the first night of their custody in court cells, without even a bed.

Prisons have made less progress in tackling bullying and intimidation. The 2000 murder of Zahid Mubarek by his cellmate at Feltham YOI illustrated this at its most extreme, and there have been other prisoner on prisoner murders. We have expressed particular concern about the safety of prisoners (and staff) in some private sector prisons, where the rapid turnover, and low number, of staff can mean that there are inexperienced staff in charge of very experienced prisoners – with the consequence that staff do not know how to, or cannot, set proper boundaries and challenge inappropriate behaviour. Again, prison overcrowding threatens the delicate balance of prison, with staff less likely to know and relate to their prisoners, and prisoners less likely to have access to positive work and activity. Prisons are only safe places because staff work very hard to keep them that way, and because most prisoners have an investment in a safe environment. If either of those breaks down, the consequences are serious. Those risks are particularly acute at the moment, with increased numbers and stretched staff and regimes.

The Joint Parliamentary Committee on Human Rights, in its 2004 report 'Deaths in custody', reiterated the Inspectorate's frequently expressed view that prevention depends not on processes but on the whole environment.

> At the level of the day to day operation of prisons and other places of detention, the culture of a prison, the extent to which people are treated with dignity, the quality of relationships between prisoners and staff, are all critically important. This is reflected in the standard against which the Chief Inspector of Prisons inspects, of a 'healthy prison', which meets standards of decency, safety and respect. This

culture is fundamental to prisoner safety and therefore to the protection of rights under Article 2 of the European Convention on Human Rights.[5]

That brings me on to the second test, respect. The culture of a prison is key to its safety, but is also key to ensuring that prisoners' human dignity is respected. In 2006 I visited some prisons in Texas. They have, I was told, improved considerably since a Federal Court case brought in an element of judicial oversight and monitoring. But the extremely limited staffing levels (one prison officer in a dormitory of 144 women; two staff for 140 maximum security men) mean that safety can only be ensured by extensive use of administrative segregation for anyone with challenging behaviour. I saw men and women who had been held in solitary confinement for up to eight years, without any positive interventions or human interaction. That is simply inhumane containment.

Our prison system in England and Wales has improved the way in which it deals with the most serious and challenging offenders. Inspection reports into the close supervision centres (used for those who have killed or seriously injured others in prison) have helped to modify the regime from one that was essentially punitive to one that aims to work and make progress with even the most dangerous prisoners. Our thematic report into high security segregation units (where there had been serious concerns about abuse, and where, in 2004, all self-inflicted deaths in high security prisons took place) recorded considerable culture change in some of those that had raised the greatest concern – though these forms of extreme custody always need the most rigorous monitoring, as they can deteriorate even more swiftly than they progress.

One of the underlying issues revealed by both this and the safer custody initiatives is the extent of mental illness within prisons. It is something that we point to again and again in inspection reports; and we have now carried out a major thematic review.[6] Healthcare in general in prisons has improved greatly, not least because, as the Inspectorate recommended in the 1990s, it is now provided by the National Health Service, the aim being to provide an equivalent standard of care to that provided anywhere else. But the availability of mental healthcare in the community, and in secure mental hospitals, is still wholly inadequate. The closure of the large mental hospitals did not, as promised, lead to 'care in the community'; it has led to care in custody. More resources have been brought in to try to deal with this, but they can only skim the surface of the most acute need. In any event there is a real danger that importing more mental healthcare into prisons sends the message that prison is the right place to treat the mentally ill – while in fact a prison can never be a therapeutic environment, and as such quite rightly cannot compulsorily treat a patient. Staff therefore see prisoners getting more ill. One man in a segregation unit was in a body-belt as otherwise he repeatedly tried to self-castrate. At Feltham YOI, the healthcare centre was entirely full of mentally ill young men, some of them suicidal and in strip clothing, being watched for twenty-four hours a day through a gate by agency nurses. This is an area where the two tests of safety and respect can collide; but such a collision reveals the fundamental flaw of using prison to contain, not to treat, mental illness.

Some prisons, particularly local prisons, have suffered a great deal from negative cultures. They have poor staff-prisoner relationships, founded on the convenience, ignorance or even abusive behaviour of staff. That is rarer now than it was, not least because the Prison Service itself has focused very strongly on decency; and prisons in general are much better managed than they used to be. But I have still been in prisons where prisoners spend far too much time in their cells, are referred to as 'bodies', or are sworn at in the hearing of inspectors. And we have come across allegations of physical abuse of prisoners in segregation, which the prisons concerned had not swiftly and properly investigated. Nevertheless, these are exceptions. More often we find prison staff struggling against the odds to manage an ever-increasing and often challenging population.

One area which continues to cause us concern is race. In spite of two investigations into racism in prisons, when we survey prisoners confidentially about the experience of prison, the perceptions of black and minority ethnic prisoners, across a whole range of issues, are almost always more negative than those of white prisoners. As our 2005 thematic report into race in prisons showed, this is often due to subtle, but nevertheless obvious, racism – in the way prisoners (and indeed black staff) are spoken about and to.

Many of our prisons are old – in fact some are Grade 1 listed buildings. That brings with it a whole range of environmental problems, from rodent and cockroach infestation to wings that let in sewage, or cannot be heated to above five degrees centigrade. Though 'slopping out' (the practice of using buckets for sanitary arrangements) has in general ceased, there are still prison wings where cells lack integral sanitation, and where prisoners are reduced to using pots, or even throwing 'poo parcels' out of the window. Prisons do not want to hold people in these conditions, but overcrowding means that it is impossible to close down, or even refurbish, some of the most unsuitable accommodation. And we had an extreme example of that in early 2007, when a wing at Norwich prison, which we had declared and the Prison Service had agreed was unfit for habitation, was emptied in order to be demolished, and on the following day was filled up again with prisoners. Shortly afterwards, however, it was permanently closed on health and safety grounds. Other mothballed accommodation is being looked at, and accommodation that was scheduled to close and be refurbished is continuing in use. Similarly, as I have said, because of overcrowding it is very common to find two prisoners sharing a cell meant for one, with an unscreened toilet, on which one of them has to sit while they eat their meals. I cannot think of any other public place where this would be tolerated on health and safety grounds.

Our third healthy prison test is purposeful activity. This is crucial, both for prisoners themselves and for society as a whole. Over 70 per cent of prisoners come into prison with literacy and numeracy levels that are below the 'employability' threshold. This is often because they lack schooling, rather than intelligence, though some do have undiagnosed or untreated learning disabilities, such as dyslexia or attention deficit disorder. Our surveys of under-eighteens in prison find that nearly half of girls in prison have been in care, and over 80 per cent of boys have been excluded from school; in one establishment, 96 per cent said they had been excluded. The consequence is that most prisoners have no experience of steady work; around two-thirds of those entering prison were unemployed before they were imprisoned.

Prison therefore provides an opportunity to make good learning deficits, and to provide some of the skills and experience that will be necessary if prisoners are to get jobs on release. It is known that getting a job is the most important factor in prisoners not reoffending. In the past, much of the work available in prisons was repetitive and boring, designed to raise revenue for the prison rather than improve the skills and life chances of the prisoner. This has changed substantially over the last few years. More and better education has been introduced, focusing on basic skills, and delivered by education professionals. Budgets are provided by government departments dealing with education and skills so that they cannot be raided by a prison governor to cover other tasks. And in many prisons workshops aim to provide and accredit skills that are likely to lead to employment: plumbing, bricklaying, fork-lift truck driving. However, there is still too little activity, particularly in local prisons that hold short-sentenced prisoners. This is not helped by the fact that the statistics that prisons keep often greatly inflate the amount of activity that is available. It does not help when prisons disguise, to government ministers and others, the real problems that overcrowded prisons face in trying to provide sufficient useful occupation for prisoners.

Even in so-called training prisons, we have found that half did not provide sufficient purposeful activity. There is a particular concern about the amount of activity available for young adults, aged eighteen to twenty-one. They are among the most prolific reoffenders, yet there are insufficient resources to provide them with the skills and training they need. Vocational skills programmes are also good ways to introduce literacy and numeracy to young men who have often avoided, or been avoided by, formal education for most of their lives, and for whom sitting in a classroom is a reminder of failure and a perception of being treated as a child.

There are some extremely good programmes – the motor mechanics workshop, for example, run by Toyota at Aylesbury YOI, or the training programme run by Transco at Reading – though they are rare and reach only a few young people. These programmes provide real skills and assured and reasonably well-paid employment immediately after prison. Other activities are evidently less useful. Parc prison, a privately run establishment, was obliged by its contract to have sixty-eight prisoners in workshops, but only six were working. In 2006 I observed four young adults desultorily and slowly packing tea-bags while ten others watched: this was described to me as 'at least teaching them the work ethic'.

And once again, even these positive developments are threatened by population pressure. Training prisons have grown considerably, often holding one thousand prisoners. Each expansion threatens to stretch tight resources even more thinly, and in a prison system that is bursting at the seams it is difficult, if not impossible, to ensure that prisoners go to a prison that can meet their needs and skills deficits, rather than simply to one that has spaces.

I mentioned at the outset of this essay that prison systems throughout Europe are having to cope with longer sentences, as capital punishment disappears. These sentences are often indeterminate, and nowhere has there been such a dramatic increase in these kinds of sentence as in the United Kingdom, despite the fact that we effectively abolished capital punishment over forty years ago. England and Wales have more indeterminate-sentenced prisoners than any other European country, a figure which expanded hugely as a result of the 2005 introduction of indefinite sentences for public protection (IPP) which could be passed on anyone who had committed a dangerous, serious or violent offence and who was thought to be at risk of doing it again. These sentences may have a relatively short minimum period of imprisonment; but at the end of this, prisoners will only be released if they can show the Parole Board that they have addressed the risk that led to their sentence in the first place. There was no national planning for how these prisoners were to be managed. In an overcrowded prison system, almost all of them were initially in practice stuck in local prisons, unable to access the courses and programmes they needed in order to address risk, and likely to stay in prison long beyond their minimum term. For the first time ever, there are more indeterminate-sentenced prisoners in our prisons than those serving less than twelve months. They are both a casualty and a cause of prison overcrowding; and a significant in-built driver to further population growth. Their presence, and frustration, has raised the risk level in the prisons where they are held.

Resettlement, our fourth test, has developed considerably since my tenure as Chief Inspector began in 2001. It is now accepted as part of the core business of prisons; indeed the whole basis of the National Offender Management Service (NOMS) is that there should be active case management of each individual prisoner, during and after imprisonment. This was something that was recommended in a joint thematic report by the Prisons and Probation inspectorates in 2001. Voluntary sector organisations and statutory employment and social security bodies have been brought into prisons to try to meet housing, employment, debt and drug treatment needs once prisoners are released. NOMS has a very ambitious target, to reduce reoffending by 10 per cent by 2010, which would indeed be a major contribution to public protection.

All this is welcome, and it is particularly welcome that prisoners' needs as people, rather than just offenders, are being recognised. But once again this is taking place against the huge pressure of a population that is expanding, and where prisoners are less and less likely to be held in or near their home areas. This is particularly true for women and young people, for whom there are fewer prisons. We have seen under-eighteens from the south-east going to Staffordshire. Young adults from London are likely to find themselves on Portland Bill. There is no women's prison at all in the West Midlands, the country's second largest conurbation, and no women's closed training prison in the north of England. This makes planning through sentence, and after sentence, all the more difficult.

And the sheer pressure of numbers, particularly of short-sentenced prisoners in local prisons, makes it almost impossible to construct and deliver individual custody plans. At best, prisoners' immediate needs on reception will be identified, and at release a jobcentre interview arranged, and some form of accommodation found, though it will often be hostel accommodation that exposes them to an environment where drug-dealing and drug-taking are normalised. Given the chaotic and dysfunctional lives of many such prisoners, this is not nearly enough, and it is scarcely surprising that a majority will return. Indeed, prison can be a refuge for those who cannot easily cope outside. I have met prisoners who committed offences because they desperately needed help with drug addiction. I also had an extremely sad letter from the mother of an autistic young man, whose support in the community ran out once he reached adulthood, and who only felt safe in the ordered environment of a prison. Once out, he would attack a policeman in the knowledge that he would return to custody. His mother was terrified that one day he would hurt some vulnerable member of the public.

In some ways, resettlement is key to understanding what prisons can and cannot do. They can only be as good as what precedes them and what follows them. Many of the people I see in prison were excluded from, or on the margins of, society long before they were literally excluded in prison. Indeed, in many ways, prisons are a microcosm of what is going wrong in the rest of society: failures in education, family life, and mental health provision; the absence of employment chances for young unskilled men. There is no simple solution to the multiple problems and marginal lifestyles that many people have acquired before they enter prison. It involves considerable investment of time and resources, often more than once. It would be far better to put in that investment at an earlier stage, before a pattern of offending has been established, and to explore robust and effective alternatives to prison for those whose problems stem from mental illness and drug dependence.

The inspection of immigration detention

I want also to discuss our work in inspecting immigration detention, an issue that Amnesty International has also taken a great interest in. Immigration detention raises particular human rights concerns. Unlike any other form of detention, it is not subject to automatic judicial oversight; it is a purely administrative decision, often taken at a fairly junior level. It also has no time limit. The Asylum and Immigration Act 1999 attempted to place some safeguards on this power, first, by requiring immigration detainees to be brought before a court within seven days, and thereafter every twenty-eight days, and secondly by giving the Prisons Inspectorate the statutory duty and power to inspect immigration removal centres (IRCs). However, only one of those safeguards, that of independent inspection, was implemented, and the automatic bail hearings provision was subsequently repealed. So inspection is the only automatic independent check and monitor of a system that has been detaining around thirty thousand adults and over two thousand children each year. Since 1999, and partly because of Opcat, our statutory remit has been extended to cover short-term holding facilities (STHFs) (often at ports, airports or immigration reporting centres) and immigration escorts.

My remit in these places is a limited one, as it is for prisons: to report on the conditions and treatment of those in detention, and not to validate the decision to detain. Nevertheless, it shines a light on an otherwise hidden system. Our methodology for inspecting IRCs and STHFs draws heavily on that which we use for prisons. The four key tests – safety, respect, purposeful activity and preparation for release or removal – are equally valid and necessary to protect the human rights of those detained. Hearing directly and in confidence from detainees, in their own language, is an essential component of inspection, as is the power to turn up at any time, without warning.

A high proportion of immigration detainees report feeling unsafe. But the reasons for this are different from those in prison. Detainees' insecurity is primarily to do with uncertainty and fear about their future, compounded by the difficulty of getting any up-to-date information on their cases and the near impossibility of getting independent competent legal advice. Our examination of case files shows that decisions to detain, and reviews of detention, rarely provide detailed reasons, specific to the individual – as would, of course, be necessary if detention automatically had to be justified before a court. Detainees therefore rarely know why they have been detained, and what will happen to them next, and when.

One of our other main concerns has been to ensure that there are effective safer custody procedures in operation. When we first began inspecting, suicide and self-harm were very rare in IRCs; they are now more common. Indeed, self-harm incidents nearly doubled between 2005 and 2006, from 858 to 1,500, and there were seven apparently self-inflicted deaths in IRCs in the two years to 2006. We have recorded concerns about the way that some suicidal detainees are managed: for example, in Oakington, where they were held in what was effectively a segregation unit. We are also particularly concerned about the rise in self-harm among foreign nationals, some of whom have served their sentences; some are desperate to go home, while others are desperate to stay here with families.

There are particular human rights issues that arise in connection with detainees who have been victims of torture or trauma before detention. Under the Detention Centre Rules, a history of torture, or of mental disorder, should render an individual unfit for detention, and therefore suitable for release.[7] We have found medical staff ill-equipped to recognise signs of torture, or to deal with its consequences. We have also found that, if the signs are recognised, and reported to the immigration authorities, no action is taken: indeed, until recently there was rarely even a response. Mental health provision and support has been inadequate in all of the centres we have inspected.

A second major human rights concern is the detention of children. As with adults, my remit is to report on their treatment and conditions, and inspections have succeeded in putting in place some important child protection safeguards, and additional education provision, for those children who are detained. But that is hardly the point. Our inspections reveal the damage that detention itself does to children, and the inadequacy of any consideration of their interests before or during detention.

The UK entered a reservation to the United Nations *Convention on the Rights of the Child* (CRC) in relation to the operation of immigration law, so that the rights of children are not paramount; but it has recently said that it will withdraw the reservation. In any event, I do not believe that children's rights and welfare needs are wholly extinguished. In the same way that the courts have held that the 1989 Children Act applies also to children in prison, this must surely be the case for children in detention. Yet we find, when we look at the process of detention, that children are in effect invisible; their needs are not even considered as part of the reasoning that decides whether detention is necessary and proportional. Inspections have revealed children taken into detention days or weeks before public examinations, or suffering from mental and physical conditions which make detention unacceptable. When we surveyed children, their comments on the process and consequences of detention showed its effects vividly:

> When they came to the house like an earthquake the way they knock. I think there were ten of them spread all around our house. They handcuffed me and my Mum through Terminal 4, through public area and into the van. My two hands were cuffed in front; I was crying in the van. That is why I just stay in my room – I keep thinking about the handcuffs.

> At the roll count they keep coming into your room and you don't know what they are going to do – you could be sleeping. Brother [ten] fell out of bed because he was scared.

The officers are tall and scary – their shoes are big and noisy. It is like a prison – I
have never killed anyone.

Detention will inevitably have a detrimental effect on a child, and, for that
reason, we expect that it will be used exceptionally, and only for the shortest
possible period. This is clearly not the case. We have also recommended that there
be independent assessments of a child's welfare and developmental needs – both
at the point of detention, and at frequent reviews thereafter – using the Children
Act test of 'risk of significant harm', and there is now a social worker in place at
Yarl's Wood, the main centre for detaining children. It has yet to be seen whether
her reports are effective, and make a difference not only to children's treatment in
detention, but to their detention *per se*.

In most centres, we have found reasonable, and sometimes good, relationships
between staff and detainees, though sometimes this is not underpinned by
sufficient understanding of cultural and religious difference. The exception was
Harmondsworth, where our 2006 inspection unusually revealed that detainees' main
fears related to staff attitudes and behaviour. This was expressed in the over-use of
force and segregation, unnecessary security measures (like confiscation of the nail
clippers) and also in the way detainees were talked to, and talked about. None of
the internal checks and monitoring systems had identified the extent, or the true
nature, of the problem. Since our inspection, there has been a change in the centre's
management – as well as a riot – and we have recorded improvements.

Given the anxieties and vulnerability of those detained, it is important that
detainees are able to be purposefully occupied. When we began our inspections,
many complained of boredom, adding to depression. Most centres have now put
in place more activities, including education, and it is now legally possible for detainees
to engage in paid work in the centres, such as cooking, cleaning and gardening,
which will also allow them to take some responsibility for their own lives and
environment. This is still slow to develop, and we are monitoring it closely.

Finally, detainees need to be properly prepared for whatever happens next.
This has not been the case so far. There is little welfare support, to help detainees
sort out the practical problems arising from unexpected detention, and to settle
their affairs if they are going to be removed. Removal itself has often been effected
without any warning, though earlier notification is now required. This has
sometimes resulted in force needing to be used on reluctant returnees who have
not had time to prepare themselves for what is to happen. This is humiliating, unsafe
and can result in serious injury. Moreover, it is neither humane nor effective, as it
often means that removal cannot in the end take place, as airlines will not accept
disruptive passengers.

In many ways, the treatment of foreign national prisoners and immigration
detainees by the immigration authorities is symptomatic of a system that deals in

case files and pieces of paper, rather than people. Few of those making decisions to detain or remove actually see the people whose lives they are affecting. Detainees can be passed around like parcels around the detention estate; we have come across detainees who have been held in six or seven different locations. Inspection humanises this process, reporting on the actual experiences of those affected.

Most recently, our inspections have lifted the veil on one of the most hidden parts of immigration detention: short-term holding facilities, which are sometimes in the controlled zone of ports and airports. They are often the first, and last, place of detention, for people who have just arrived, or are being removed, and who are therefore at their most vulnerable. Inspections revealed environments that were often wholly unsuitable holding men, women and children, sometimes overnight in rooms that lacked beds, bedding or even enough heat. The most extreme were the so-called 'dog kennels' in Calais, which would probably have been condemned as unfit by animal welfare organisations had they been used for that purpose. By contrast, and perhaps surprisingly, we have found staff in most of those centres to be generally sympathetic to the situation and stress of detainees. Indeed in one centre staff out of their own pockets had furnished a room for children. We are more worried about the treatment of detainees on escorts, where force is sometimes used on reluctant and sometimes panicky detainees, and where it is very difficult to establish what has occurred, since those detainees have often been removed.

In all these settings, independent inspection is a vital part of the protection of the human rights of those in custody. Of course, it can only work if the custodians, too, are signed up to those values. The Prisons Inspectorate has no regulatory or executive power, which is an inevitable consequence of the fact that we do not simply invigilate the standards, under current resources, of prisons and immigration centres. It is a credit to those running our prisons that, since 2001, there have been measurable improvements in all four of our healthy prison tests, improvements including better and safer custody, healthcare, education and resettlement work. And when we ourselves follow up the recommendations that we make to each establishment in each inspection report, we find that over 70 per cent have been achieved, either wholly or in part. In 2006 that meant that there had been over two thousand changes in practice in prisons and IRCs. But there is still a great deal to be done.

In 2006–7, we saw some of the effects of extreme population pressure. In all the prisons most affected by overcrowding – adult male local, training and open prisons – our assessments during that period were less positive than they were in the previous twelve months. We saw local prisons sliding back or failing to improve, and training prisons where half our assessments are negative. Prisons were literally full to capacity, with prisoners sleeping in court cells, accommodation that was condemned as not fit for purpose being brought back into use, and prisoners unable to move to the prisons they needed to be in in order to decrease their risks and increase their skills. More prison places were hurriedly planned, but they were chasing ever-rising numbers.

The more new prison spaces are created, the greater the risk that already stretched resources will be spread even more thinly, while at the same time less will be available for necessary and effective interventions outside prisons.

I have often said that it is always better to build an ark before, rather than during or after the flood – and I have made clear that that ark consists not just of increased prison spaces, but of sufficient resources to work effectively with prisoners. And crucially, we need sufficient resources outside prison to deal properly with the mentally ill, with drug abusers, and with non-violent offenders (especially women and children) – both instead of and after custody. Without that, our prisons will be merely containers, recycling the same people again and again and again.

I am glad to report that plans to merge the Prisons Inspectorate with the four other criminal justice inspectorates were dropped – though it is important that we do joint work, where relevant, with partner inspectorates, such as healthcare, education, probation and police. But prisons inspection is different, involving examining in detail, robustly and independently, all that goes on behind prison walls, in the light of what should happen, rather than what necessarily does. There has never been a greater need for this work, as standards are threatened by growing numbers.

Our work has made a difference, and its importance is recognised overseas as well as in the UK. In 2006 the Correctional Services of Canada published two reports by us into women's federal prisons, and we contributed to the growing debate in the USA about prison conditions and oversight. This included my appearance before the Commission on Safety and Abuse in America's Prisons, which concluded, as one of its four key recommendations of its 2006 report 'Confronting confinement':

> The most important mechanism for overseeing corrections is independent inspection and monitoring. Every prison and jail should be monitored by an independent government body, sufficiently empowered and funded to regularly inspect conditions of confinement and report findings to lawmakers and the public.[8]

Our work was cited as a leading example of such independent scrutiny. It is clear that it will be even more crucial in the future than it has been in the past.

Notes

1 Editor's note: this essay was written in February 2007; figures cited apply as at 2007.
2 The text is available at www2.ohchr.org/english/law/cat-one.htm (accessed 28 February 2009).

3 *Expectations: Criteria for Assessing the Conditions in Prisons and the Treatment of Prisoners* (Her Majesty's Inspectorate of Prisons, 2006), available at http://inspectorates.homeoffice. gov.uk/hmiprisons/docs/expectations-2008?view=Binary (accessed 14 February 2009).
4 HMIP reviews can be found at http://inspectorates.justice.gov.uk/hmiprisons/ (accessed 14 February 2009).
5 Available via www.publications.parliament.uk/pa/jt200405/jtselect/jtrights/15/1502.htm (accessed 15 February 2009).
6 Editor's note: this review resulted in the report 'The mental health of prisoners: thematic review of the care and support of prisoners with mental health needs' (Her Majesty's Inspectorate of Prisons, 2007).
7 The Detention Centre Rules, Statutory Instrument 2001 No. 238 (The Stationery Office), available at www.opsi.gov.uk/SI/si2001/20010238.htm (accessed 15 February 2009).
8 'Confronting confinement: a report of the Commission on Safety and Abuse in America's Prisons' (New York: Vera Institute of Justice, 2006), available via www. prisoncommission.org/report.asp (accessed 15 February 2009).

1a   Liora Lazarus

Inspecting the tail of the dog[1]

Her Majesty's Inspectorate of Prisons is one of the few success stories of the United Kingdom penal system in the post-war period. Since its establishment the post has been held by a number of stridently independent and brave critics of the penal conditions of convicted offenders, as well as immigrant detainees. The independence of the Inspectorate has been maintained, despite the close institutional nexus between the Inspectorate and the Home Office: a nexus which was severely tested when the Home Secretary, Michael Howard, came to blows with Stephen Tumim in the mid-1990s. In many ways, the Inspectorate is a shining example of how British constitutionalism works at its best: where conventions of independence and integrity are maintained, lived out and respected in practice without the strict framework of rules or institutional separation. It is because of this uncompromising rigour and independence that the Commission on Safety and Abuse in America's Prisons called upon the UK's Prisons Inspectorate as a possible way forward for improving oversight and accountability in US prisons (and, importantly, those within US occupied territory).

Needless to say, the UK Inspectorate's practice of independence has not only been bolstered by the practice of the individuals who hold its office, or the constitutional conventions of which I speak here. It is also, as Anne Owers indicates, increasingly able to rely on practices, institutions and norms, developed at the international and regional level. The UN Committee Against Torture (CAT) and the European Committee for the Prevention of Torture and Inhuman or Degrading Treatment or Punishment (CPT) were both established by treaty in the late 1980s. More recently, the *Optional Protocol to the UN Convention against Torture* (Opcat) requires signatory states to institute inspectorate mechanisms in their jurisdictions. All of these developments strengthen the safeguards necessary for the continuing independence of the UK Inspectorate, but also inform their normative outlook. So it was that the most recent edition of the Inspectorate's *Expectations*, norms promoting good practice in the protection of prisoners' human rights and which form the basis for the Inspectorate's work, was able to 'draw on, and be referenced against, international human rights standards'.[2]

Anne Owers' Oxford Amnesty Lecture is a testimony to the success of her work, most visible in her development of the Inspectorate's set of *Expectations*. These now set forth a holistic human rights approach to the running of prisons centred on safety, respect, purposeful activity and resettlement. The *Expectations* provide one of the few genuinely ambitious sets of normative aspirations within the UK penal system, and should certainly form part of any statutory reform of prisoners' rights in the future. Other evidence of the importance of the Inspectorate's work is evident in Ms Owers' essay: from the highlighting and eventual reduction of prison suicides (to a slightly less alarming level than previously), and the improvement in detoxification conditions, to the exposure of the plight of immigrant detainees, and immigrant children detainees in particular.

Nevertheless, alongside these noteworthy successes, Ms Owers also tells a less optimistic story. A story of endemic overcrowding, of sub-standard physical conditions, of dangerous circumstances for mentally ill offenders, of alarming rates of self-harm in female offenders, and of tragic racist murders such as that of Zahid Mubarek. These are indications that much more needs to be done to improve conditions and respect for dignity in prisons, if the prison service is to begin to talk of meeting the Inspectorate's 'expectations'. It is to this less optimistic tale that I would like to turn, and to talk of some of the deeper and more intractable obstacles facing prison reform advocates in this country.

I want to talk of why it is that Anne Owers and her predecessors so often have cause for complaint. For it is not so much that prison governors, or officers, are not well meaning or hardworking, or even that those who run the prison system are not equally keen to demonstrate that they treat prisoners 'humanely, decently and lawfully'.[3] It is more than evident from Owers' words that the work of the Inspectorate and the Prison Service is radically undermined by chronic conditions of overcrowding, and the seemingly inexorable rise of the prison population. This week in August 2007 the prison population rose to 81,309, which means that we have seen a 25 per cent increase in absolute terms in the last seven years. What this trend indicates is that the penal system exists in a large and complex political and social landscape, the dynamics of which it has little control over, but the consequences of which it has to face on a daily basis.

It is because of this complexity that I want to talk about the processes that lie behind this state of affairs – to allude to a broader political and social context which has generated a politics of crime control and insecurity, of 'populist punitivism' and a 'governance through crime'.[4] I also want to talk about the absence of a robust human rights culture which could potentially stem the inexorable progress towards a mass incarcerative society, or help us to generate more fundamental statutory reform of prisoners' rights. I want to argue that these two processes co-exist – a culture of control and a politics of rights scepticism – in a particular way to undermine the objectives of penal reform and prisoners' rights. For no matter how essential the Inspectorate is to the individual lives of prisoners (and in some cases the Inspectorate can claim to have saved the lives of prisoners), and no matter how imaginative the Inspectorate has been in the development of expectations which place prisons and prison standards in a broader context, its institutional effectiveness will inevitably be limited to inspecting the tail of the dog. I want to talk about the dog that wags that tail.

Let us begin with the dynamics of criminal justice policy within a politics of 'insecurity'. Most criminologists and sociologists of crime agree that advanced democracies are now characterised by a political preoccupation with avoiding risk and containing danger.[5] This preoccupation is further fuelled – and politically exploited – by the social perception of 'insecurity'. These conditions have been described by David Garland as constituting the aspects of a 'culture of control'. That is a culture that accepts high crime rates as a normal social fact; where popular anxiety about crime, and declining social sympathy, are commonplace; crime is politicised and emotively represented; victims' rights and public safety concerns dominate at the expense of offender rights and the civil liberties of the population at large; and crime consciousness is institutionalised by the media and popular culture.[6] Such a culture creates the preconditions for punitiveness and the intensified use of the criminal law in the management of society or, to borrow from Jonathan Simon, 'governing through crime'.[7]

Control of crime has thus become a central strategic and symbolic factor in the exercise of political authority, to the extent that its use is now deployed to legitimate political strategies which often fall outside the traditional ambit of the criminal law. One need only look at the plethora of hybrid criminal-civil measures, such as control and anti-social behaviour orders, to see that the human rights standard of 'no crime without law' no longer clearly defines the realm of the criminal. Equally, crime, and its prevention, has now captured in its wake territories which previously would have been understood as the province of the welfare state. Thus, under the Labour Government, the way families are managed, or childhood is experienced, has shifted from the province of schools and social services to that of multi-agency teams aimed at the prevention of youth crime. Such a process of governing through crime flourishes in a politics of insecurity[8] – a political exploitation of our feelings or anxieties about crime and our failure to control or know the world around us – a politics which has now taken on quite another dimension since the so-called 'war on terror' began.

Chasing security, within a politics of insecurity, produces a spiral of anxiety, where, despite more laws being enacted in its pursuit, security remains unattained and continuously unfulfilled. Because the conditions of its legitimation require a constant exploitation of our fears, the security state is an endlessly hungry beast whose appetite can, by necessity, never be sated. Structurally, this combination leads to an ongoing extension of the criminal law's reach. This explains why, in the ten years since the Blair Government's accession, we have seen fifty-three Acts of Parliament on crime and punishment enacted, ten more than the forty-three pieces of criminal justice legislation enacted in the preceding one hundred years.[9] While it is difficult to isolate a direct causal relationship between the number of crimes enacted and the number of people in prison, there can be little doubt that increasing criminalisation has a considerable bearing on the trajectory of the prison population.

This climate is also dangerously antipathetic to the rights of those suspected and convicted of committing crimes. Casting defendant and prisoner rights in opposition to the attainment of security is now ubiquitous in political rhetoric, as in David Cameron's assertion that 'the Human Rights Act has introduced a culture that has inhibited law enforcement and the supervision of convicted criminals'.[10] Moreover, the arguments are becoming increasingly more sophisticated and subtle. Thus, the former Home Secretary, John Reid, in May 2007 gave a security-based attack, founding his speech on the assertion that the 'the right to security, to the protection of life and liberty, is and should be the basic right on which all others are based'.[11] This was an assertion not about fundamental rights, but an attempt to create a normative legitimation in order to undermine rights, by casting security as a meta-right: a right which grounds, and by implication trumps, all other rights.

It should come as no surprise to us then, that in her attempt to capture the complex rhetoric of insecurity politics for better objectives, Anne Owers finds herself arguing that:

> It has been suggested that human rights and public protection are in opposition to one another; and that over-concern with human rights can result in damage to the safety of the public. I would very strongly refute that. Public protection – the ability of people to live in safety, without threats to their life and well-being – is itself a core human right. The state therefore has a positive duty to do all it can to protect the life and human dignity of the public, as well as prison staff and prison officers. That means that prisons must be safe places which contribute actively to public protection, by making it less, rather than more, likely that those incarcerated will reoffend once released.

In today's climate, the strategic force of Owers' language here is unassailable. What better way to launch a plea for prisoners' humanity and for positive prison regimes than to harness the prevailing political rhetoric of public protection, and even the 'right to public protection'? Nevertheless, it is important to be alert to the implications of this type of persuasive strategy. For one, the argument for positive regimes here rests in large part on the instrumental goal of crime reduction, not on prisoners' intrinsic humanity and potential (even if unrealised). The point is, from a non-instrumental perspective, it should be possible to argue for the rights of a persistently recidivist offender – or even an offender who cannot be rehabilitated.

Moreover, even from a strategic or instrumental perspective, crime reduction – in a political culture which both fosters and exploits fear of crime – constitutes a precarious basis upon which to ground the protection of prisoners' rights. What happens if crime isn't reduced, or isn't seen to be reduced, and fear of crime keeps rising despite positive regimes in prisons? Do we make them harsher instead?

We need also to find new critical perspectives on the rhetoric of 'public protection' which can capture the public imagination and militate against the spiralling pursuit of security. This isn't necessarily done, as Owers does here, by marrying the discourse of rights with the discourse of security or public protection – and creating a right to security. Instead, perhaps we need also to launch a claim for a right to insecurity. If such a right is to exist it is a right to a life of self-creation, of unknowns, of surprise and necessary risk, of fission and, most importantly, of freedom. For if we are to live in a society where the right to security becomes the meta-right upon which we legitimate claims to all other social values, we will, inevitably, undermine the freedom which we hold dear. The point is, with freedom comes risk and insecurity; it is a necessary concomitant of the liberal society.[12]

But why is it that Owers has to harness security and public protection as a way to legitimate the rights claims of prisoners, rather than calling upon traditional rights arguments to counter the prevailing politics of insecurity? Why is it that rights don't constitute politically animating claims in and of themselves? The answer lies in the politics, or even culture, of rights scepticism in this country. Rights-sceptical politics in the United Kingdom is a curious mixture of a misplaced Europhobia,[13] left wing and communitarian antipathy to the egotistic individualism of rights talk and the elitism of the judges who decide on rights, conservative pragmatic dislike of categorical idealism, and critical legal realist arguments that point to the gap between rights talk and their realisation on the ground. Rights scepticism is rooted also in the strong tradition of political majoritarianism in English constitutional orthodoxy and its utilitarian underpinnings. That is not to say that the UK does not have a culture of liberty, one in which the common law has incrementally protected the negative freedoms that the law has permitted us to retain. But rights, as positive articulations of idealistic notions such as human dignity, do not roll off the tongue in English constitutional vernacular.

The consequence then, is that when we are faced with one of the very real tensions at the centre of liberal democracies – the balance between security and rights – we are left without a robust rights culture which can counter the tide of majoritarian political claims. We are left therefore in a world where 'our freedoms' are distinguished from 'their rights', where 'popular rights' are pitted against 'minority rights', and where political capital is gained from doing so. Thus it is that David Cameron can claim, 'I believe it is wrong to undermine public safety – and indeed public confidence in the concept of human rights – by allowing highly dangerous criminals and terrorists to trump the rights of the people of Britain to live in security and peace.'[14]

It is in this precarious moral world of insecurity politics and rights scepticism that advocates for prisoners' rights, Anne Owers chief among them, must tentatively advance their claims for penal reform. One where, as Ian Loader argues, 'political, professional and media actors are able to mobilise a populist appeal to the idea of security, while presenting rights claims as the concern of remote special interest groups willing to play fast and loose with the safety of their co-citizens'.[15] This is the world that frustrates attempts to reduce the scourge of prison overcrowding, or even of penal warehousing. It is this dog that wags the tail of the penal system, and it is this dog that barks outside the Prison Inspectorate's door. While reading this essay by the Chief Inspector of Prisons perhaps we, as ordinary participants in the democratic process, need to think more about how we can challenge this increasingly pervasive discourse of insecurity, and how to recharge rights claims in a utilitarian political culture where tramping on rights now symbolises, for an increasingly anxious population, that something is being done about security.

Notes

1 Editor's note: this response was written on 7 August 2007; figures pertain to that date.
2 *Expectations: Criteria for Assessing the Conditions in Prisons and the Treatment of Prisoners* (Her Majesty's Inspectorate of Prisons, 2006), p. 1.
3 HM Prison Service, Statement of Purpose, www.hmprisonservice.gov.uk/abouttheservice/statementofpurpose/ (accessed 7 August 2007).
4 These concepts emerge, in particular, in the work of Anthony Bottoms and Jonathan Simon, respectively.
5 I distinguish between the conditions of advanced democracies and developing democracies (or transitional societies) for this purpose. There is a noticeable difference between the UK and South Africa for example, in that perception of the threat of crime is far closer to its actual incidence in South Africa than it is in the UK.
6 David Garland, *The Culture of Control* (Oxford: Oxford University Press, 2001).
7 Jonathan Simon, *Governing through Crime* (Oxford: Oxford University Press, 2007).
8 Richard Ericson, *Crime in an Insecure World* (Cambridge: Polity Press, 2007).
9 See Ian Loader, 'This internment lobby risks harming not just liberty, but security itself' *Guardian* (20 July 2007), p. 37. www.guardian.co.uk/commentisfree/2007/jul/20/comment.terrorism (accessed 26 February 2009).
10 Speech to Centre for Policy Studies, 26 June 2006, available at www.guardian.co.uk/politics/2006/jun/26/conservatives.constitution (accessed 9 July 2009).
11 Speech reported on http://news.bbc.co.uk/2/hi/uk_news/politics/6648849.stm, 12 May 2007 (accessed 26 February 2009).
12 For those who think that to argue for a right to insecurity is frivolous in times such as these, perhaps it is more palatable to argue for constraints on the right to security, or public protection. In short, the right to security cannot amount to the right to be secure. Instead it should constitute a narrower right to be free from identifiable and reasonably foreseeable risks of gross harm or violence to person. In this way, at least

the obligation which falls on the state in order to protect its citizens against such violence is delimited, realisable and identifiable. Moreover, because such an obligation doesn't allow for pre-emptive state action on the basis of unknown future risks, it is more likely to be consistent with individual autonomy.

13 Given the historical role that the UK played in the drafting of the *European Convention on Human Rights*, it has always been somewhat mysterious as to why it is that we find headlines such as 'British law should not be undermined by these Euro outsiders; human rights ruling destroys our freedom', *Express* (7 May 2001).

14 Speech to Centre for Policy Studies, 26 June 2006. As note 10, above.

15 Ian Loader, 'The cultural lives of security and rights', in B. Goold and L. Lazarus (eds), *Security and Human Rights* (Oxford: Hart, 2007).

2 Shami Chakrabarti

Asylum and incarceration[1]

While I was preparing this essay, the poem 'Refugee Blues' by W. H. Auden kept coming into mind.[2] I love this poem, with its lament for home that 'We cannot go there now, my dear', because it reminds me of how our modern notions of human rights came about and why the plight of the refugee is at their heart. Bizarrely, and to an extent I would never have imagined even twenty years ago, we are in desperate need of such reminders in Britain today.

We have quite simply lost our way – lost sight of a moral compass agreed upon across the globe in the wake of the Holocaust and the Second World War. Sure enough we all suffer a little from this amnesia as to why human rights matter. As compassion is replaced with complacency and principle with permanent exception, we begin to jeopardise even the rights of the many. But in this more brutal Britain, none are so vulnerable as asylum seekers, and incarcerated asylum seekers in particular.

The very notion of asylum has been denigrated by populist politics in thought, word and deed. And this is not just far right politics but that of Government and mainstream opposition. Further, asylum seekers have been demonised in parts of the media and, perhaps more startlingly, under-protected by law. The result is that we lock up far too many of these desperate and vulnerable people. We lock them up for far too long, in some cases up to five years. We lock them up with their children. We lock up lone children with adult strangers (while we argue about their true age). We lock up victims of unlawful past imprisonment, and of rape and torture. We provide inadequate reasons for this imprisonment when our true reasons are often administrative convenience and political expediency. We provide inadequate access to lawyers and courts. We welcome too many of those coming to our shores seeking safe-haven, not with asylum but incarceration. We punish those seeking refuge so as to deter others from doing the same. This is the reality of Britain's 'ethical foreign policy' and border control at the start of the twenty-first century: we are breaking a promise, reneging on the world's apology to the victims of the

Holocaust, and beginning to deny and dismantle the framework once built in their name.

Dictionary definitions of 'refugee' and 'asylum' present a positive or at least neutral picture of a person in flight from war, persecution or natural disaster, and seeking shelter or protection by a receiving state, while in our linguistic heritage the words have a very broad relation to flight and protection. In the legal definition given by the United Nations' 1951 *Convention Relating to the Status of Refugees* (the Refugee Convention) a refugee is one who:

> owing to a well-founded fear of being persecuted for reasons of race, religion, nationality, membership of a particular social group or political opinion, is outside the country of his nationality and is unable, or owing to such fear, is unwilling to avail himself of the protection of that country.[3]

Article 33 of the same Convention contains the vital obligation against return ('refoulement') of refugees to places of danger. This principle of non-refoulement has enjoyed a place in English statute law since at least the Extradition Act of 1870. Further, Article 31 recognises the logic that it will often be the neediest escaping exile who must employ means such as forged papers and illegal entry. It therefore prohibits penalising them for these methods of escape as long as they come directly from the country of persecution, present themselves to the authorities without delay, and show good cause for their illegal entry or presence.

Article 5 of the *European Convention on Human Rights and Fundamental Freedoms* is of course now a central feature of the British Human Rights Act of 1998.[4] It is our local, modern reflection of the ancient right against arbitrary detention, originally encapsulated in the writ of *habeas corpus*. It applies to everyone in our country, regardless of nationality or other status. (And as we have recently celebrated the bicentenary of the abolition of the slave trade in England, it is worth remembering how *habeas corpus* came to the abolitionists' aid and freed a slave in the famous *Somersett's Case* of 1772.)

Article 5 provides that:

> Everyone has the right to liberty and security of person. No one shall be deprived of his liberty save in the following cases and in accordance with a procedure prescribed by law:
> a) the lawful detention of a person after conviction by a competent court;
> b) the lawful arrest or detention of a person for non-compliance with the lawful order of a court or in order to secure the fulfilment of any obligation prescribed by law;
> c) the lawful arrest or detention of a person effected for the purpose of bringing him before the competent legal authority on reasonable suspicion of having committed an offence or when it is reasonably considered necessary to prevent his committing an offence or fleeing after having done so;

d) the detention of a minor by lawful order for the purpose of educational supervision or his lawful detention for the purpose of bringing him before the competent legal authority;

e) the lawful detention of persons for the prevention of the spreading of infectious diseases, of persons of unsound mind, alcoholics or drug addicts or vagrants;

f) the lawful arrest or detention of a person to prevent his effecting an unauthorised entry into the country or of a person against whom action is being taken with a view to deportation or extradition.

Crucially, this is an exhaustive list of justifications for detention in a democratic society. The final immigration control justification at Article 5.1(f) is simple and precise: detention must be either to prevent illegal entry or to effect deportation. Not for administrative convenience in the asylum claims process and not to send signals to the world that asylum seekers are not welcome here. Article 5 goes on to provide that everyone arrested 'shall be informed promptly, in a language which he understands, of the reasons for his arrest and of any charge against him'. Those arrested under the suspicion of crime justification are promptly to be brought before a judge and are entitled to trial within a reasonable time or bail. Finally, everyone detained is entitled to bring speedy challenge to the lawfulness of their incarceration in court and to release and compensation in the case of unlawful detention. So much for the theory. The practice requires a little history and context.

If the 1951 Refugee Convention began as an apology, it quickly became a source of pride. The defecting athletes, ballerinas and spies of the Cold War were European heroic figures, a vindication of democratic values, reminders of the evils of Communism and the superior society that we enjoyed in the West. During this period, the focus of anti-migration sentiment and enforcement was not on refugees (the more qualified term 'asylum seeker' having yet to enter popular usage) but on mostly lawful economic migrants from the Commonwealth. In the twenty-year period leading up to 1981, Britain began closing the door on lawful non-asylum related migration from the Commonwealth as it opened the door to free trade and movement of people within Europe.[5] The tension between Britain's policy towards the Commonwealth and towards Europe is a complex one as far as human rights, migration and race relations are concerned.

On the one hand, the Council of Europe and European Union systems have been highly instrumental in the broad maintenance of both peace and democracy for well over fifty years. On the other hand, while the Commonwealth came with a somewhat embarrassing imperial back-story, it was at least a family of nations encompassing first and developing worlds and both multi-racial and multi-cultural in character.

Conversely, there is a deepening danger of a largely white, rich 'fortress Europe' that deals with its own crisis of confidence and complexity by turning on those from outside. This brings the risk (exacerbated by the efforts of British governments) that the harmonisation of asylum and human rights standards within Europe becomes a race to the bottom and not the top. If this seems fanciful, just think of how many times you have heard a justification of British poor treatment of asylum seekers on the basis of what happens in France, Germany or elsewhere. Other countries do or do not recognise certain types of persecution, do or do not make life comfortable for applicants in waiting, do or do not send people back to this or that unpleasant destination.

However, just as Britain's immigration doors began closing on much of the world, air travel was becoming cheaper and easier. The practical paradigm of the refugee escaping across a land border under cover of night was replaced with the airport tarmac asylum claim. The obligation in the Refugee Convention that those seeking its protection should do so in the first safe country remained. However, this country was now just as likely to be on the other side of the world, where the refugee may also have family, linguistic and other cultural ties borne of the imperial past.

The term 'interdependent world' is all the rage today. You rarely hear a politician's speech without reference to it. We are told that this is the justification for labelling people in Britain as 'terrorists' if they would take up arms against a dictatorship on another continent. We are told that this is the justification for military intervention in other regions, and more benignly, for greater development aid and debt forgiveness. The missing piece of this puzzle is asylum. Global interdependence justifies war and famine relief over there but not it seems, a warm welcome to the victims of such wars and famines who manage to make it over here. This is a political and emotional disconnect that began over twenty years ago.

United Kingdom Home Office folklore (which we must gather and preserve while we can), sets great store by the arrival of an airliner carrying fifty-four Sri Lankan refugees in 1986. Certainly, a subtle shift in policy can be traced to the Immigration (Carrier's Liability) Act of the following year which made carriers liable to hefty fines for bringing 'inadequately documented passengers' to our shores. For while the Refugee Convention precludes the summary removal of claimants to refugee protection, it does not expressly require the facilitation of their passage to signatory states. Further, a persecuted person does not even become a Convention refugee until he is *outside* his country of nationality.

So we began to make it just that little bit harder for escaping refugees (however genuine or desperate) to escape to Britain. Here, our island geography was a bonus. Escape by air can be undermined by placing visa regimes on countries producing large numbers of claimants. The burden of policing visas can be put on airlines by way of carriers' liability fines. Yet desperate people might still escape to the United Kingdom, perhaps buying tickets to other destinations which require a change of planes at Heathrow airport. So the 'transit visa', requiring pre-vetting before someone can even come to our transit lounges, was born. Unlike traditional visas, the transit visa has no application in relation to any class of traveller other than the asylum seeker. Who else need bother with the wasted cost of onward passage?

By 1998, the list of unwelcome refugees or nationals requiring transit visas for the United Kingdom included those from Afghanistan, the Democratic Republic of the Congo, the Federal Republic of Yugoslavia, Iran, Iraq and Zimbabwe. Here was complete dissonance between the ethics of foreign and home policy. Britain had broken faith with the Refugee.

Yet desperate people still came. Fortress Europe is not an island and is more easily achieved in rhetoric than reality. So now Government turned its attentions from obstructing the method of escape to chilling the welcome on arrival. Policies designed to discourage 'pull factors' to this country and to 'send signals about Britain not being a soft touch' were adopted. Appeals and access to legal aid have been cut back. At one point the Government even attempted completely to oust the jurisdiction of the higher courts in immigration and asylum matters.

Of course asylum seekers are not permitted to work in the UK – this being considered a prime potential 'pull factor'. So experiments in various means of asylum support descended into experiments in forced destitution, both to discourage the choice of Britain in the first place and then to encourage 'voluntary departure' at the end of the appeals process. In the latter case, even those with children were not immune. Indeed, the policy was originally 'spun' as an attempt to encourage failed asylum seekers to leave for fear that their children might be taken from them.

Then there were the policies of criminalisation. Home secretaries had long spoken of asylum and crime in the same sentences, or the same breaths of rousing conference speeches. Now the policy approaches began to merge as well. Just as foreign national terror suspects were denied their rights to criminal due process by the legal fiction of 'detention pending impossible deportation', asylum seekers became subject to fingerprinting, electronic tagging and prosecution for criminal offences such as illegal entry.

Unsurprisingly and after prolonged rhetorical and practical attacks on asylum, asylum seekers, and the law, lawyers and judges who protect them, the then Prime Minister told the Confederation of British Industry in April 2004 that 'the UN Convention on Refugees, first introduced in 1951 . . . has started to show its age'.[6]

It is against this background that one has to look at the immigration removal centres of Harmondsworth and Oakington and Dungavel. It is in this context that one has to weigh the assurances from Government that detention is only used where necessary and primarily to allow for fair and lawful removal at the end of the appeals process. This is a far cry from the reality as seen by independent watchdogs, academics, lawyers, psychiatrists and refugees and asylum seekers themselves.

In 2005 Amnesty International published the report 'Seeking asylum is not a crime', which contains the stories of many individuals, including Jean.[7] After fleeing a country where she was assaulted and raped, and her brother killed, she applied, with her seven-year-old son, for asylum in the UK. Because her country was on the 'white list' of countries considered safe, her case was fast-tracked and she and her son detained. Her asylum claim was rejected as 'clearly unfounded', with no in-country right of appeal, and her application for bail refused. Medical staff expressed concern about the mental and physical health of Jean's son, who could not go to school because he was in detention, but no action was taken. Eventually a new solicitor came on board and after 143 days Jean and her son were released from detention, granted the right to appeal their claim rejection from within the UK, and finally recognised as refugees. The report quotes Jean's distress: '"I felt so stressed. It's horrible being in detention especially with a child. My child wanted to kill himself he said 'mummy we're in prison'."'

There is so much in this short story of life as an incarcerated asylum seeker in Britain. Here a victim of torture and rape is detained with a small child. Britain maintains a sweeping reservation from the UN *Convention on the Rights of the Child* for the purposes of immigration control, thereby undermining the Government's exhortation that 'every child matters'.[8]

The psychological and medical consequences of indefinite detention are obvious and well known. They are said to be particularly bad for young children who fail to settle and thrive in such an environment which also exacerbates the mental health problems of their parents.

In the excellent if terrifying report 'No place for a child', the charity Save the Children estimated that approximately two thousand children are held in immigration detention in the UK each year.[9] There appears to be no available data on asylum seekers whose age is in dispute. Of the thirty-two children in the sample half were detained for more than twenty-eight days (the current maximum for detaining terrorist suspects without charge). The longest period of detention was 268 days – an extremely long period in the life of a child. Detention is far from limited to a last resort tool for securing removal at the end of the appeals process. People are detained at various stages in their encounter with the authorities and while families with children present a naturally low risk of evading the control, some commentators believe that these low-hanging fruit are singled out for detention.

Bail does exist in theory but without automatic bail hearings or ready access to advice and representation once incarcerated, asylum seekers are in a far worse position than those detained via the criminal arrest system, with its duty solicitors and statutory time limits. Further, the Government appears to keep scant data on this shameful and shadowy world of asylum and incarceration. But for the efforts of small charities such as Bail for Immigration Detainees and independent monitors like Her Majesty's Inspector of Prisons, Anne Owers, there would be even less information about the circumstances that lead to despair, riots and even suicides within the detention estate.

In short, the philosophy of asylum detention in this country seems to be moving further and further away from the notions of necessity, proportionality and individuated justice that are encapsulated in human rights instruments. Most worryingly, the courts at home and in Strasbourg have been slow to stem the flow. I'll consider here one important case and its implications.

The case of *Saadi v. the United Kingdom* went to the European Court of Human Rights (ECHR) via our own House of Lords Appellate Committee. It represents one of the worst compromises of hard-won due process principles in recent years. It concerned the practice of 'fast-tracking' asylum claims and detaining claimants pending consideration at Oakington detention centre (referred to as a 'reception centre').

Mr Saadi is an Iraqi Kurd who arrived in Britain at the turn of 2000 and 2001. While not central to his case, the ironic chill of his welcome to the UK should not be lost on anyone interested in the fault lines between our approach to foreign and home affairs. For the first three days he was not detained but then he was detained as an Iraqi ripe for 'fast-tracking' at Oakington. Three days after that his lawyer was told the reasons for his detention over the telephone, and notwithstanding a *refusal* of asylum, he was released four days after that.

Mr Saadi was ultimately granted refugee status. The central issue in his case before each tier of domestic court and the ECHR was whether his seven-day detention, based not on individual behaviour or other risk factors, but on an administrative system that decided to treat Iraqis as a 'job lot', was justified and lawful under Article 5.1(f) of the European Convention, the specification that detention must be to prevent illegal entry or to effect deportation. Was this detention preventing his unauthorised entry, when he had presented to the authorities at the airport and previously been granted temporary admission? Was it somehow with a view to deportation, when he'd yet even to have his claim considered?

The British High Court said no, his detention didn't meet these criteria; every other court said yes. In its majority judgment, the ECHR engaged in legal logical contortions that would never have been entertained for a non-asylum-seeking class of humanity, refusing to accept, even, that an immediate and open asylum claim at the airport was an attempt at 'authorised' (as opposed to 'unauthorised') entry.

For the ECHR in Saadi's case, it was somehow sufficient that administrative detention was part of an overall system of immigration control. Testing the necessity of an individual detention was unimportant. Article 5 was less protective of an asylum seeker's liberty than the liberty of others. When human rights courts discriminate in this way, when they ignore both the language and the purpose of the right against arbitrary detention – that right that protects men, women and

children all over the world from the midnight knock at the door and disappearance
– what will populist politicians do?

The logic of the House of Lords was that asylum seekers with pending claims
are yet to be authorised or not. If detained *en masse* for administrative processing,
some will turn out to be unauthorised, even fraudulent. Thus the detention of all
en masse can be said to be preventing unauthorised entry. Imagine such logic
applied to other types of detention. The evasion of taxes owed under law is criminal behaviour, as is giving fraudulent answers on a tax questionnaire. Imagine whole
classes of high rate tax payers detained during the completion and assessment of
tax returns on the basis that some will turn out to be lying. Justified? Lawful under
5.1(c), the criminal suspicion ground of detention? I think not. Not in the United
Kingdom, nor elsewhere in Europe, nor anywhere in the democratic world.

The Saadi case was then referred to the Grand Chamber of the ECHR, where
a majority decision was taken that there had been no violation of Article 5.1(f).[10]
Perhaps there is hope in turning the corner, though, in the minority dissenting
opinion expressed by six judges, who closed by describing asylum and immigration
as 'the most crucial issues facing us in the years to come. Is it a crime to be a
foreigner? We do not think so.'

And if the law were to stand firmer, perhaps the politics might follow? A progressive,
democratic international politics waking up to the 'interconnected' nature of
different policies and corners of the globe. Global warming must be met of course
by the cutting of carbon emissions, but also with thought for the refugees of future
dramatic climate change. Poverty and disease must of course be met by international trade and aid policy. But humanitarian cheque-books over there won't excuse
brutal checkpoints over here. And whether or not human rights abuse
overseas becomes a more legitimate justification for war, those wars and the
movements of people that ensue cannot justify human rights abuses against
asylum seekers in the United Kingdom.

We require something more than a 'lock them out or lock them up' approach
to the world's refugees. The present path is too damaging to our social, legal and
moral systems; to our humanity.

Notes

1 Editor's note: this essay was revised in February 2008.
2 W. H. Auden, *Collected Shorter Poems, 1927–1957* (London: Faber and Faber, 1966).
3 Article 1; text of the Refugee Convention available at www2.ohchr.org/english/law/
   refugees.htm (accessed 16 February 2009).
4 For the text of the European Convention, see 'basic texts' available via www.echr.
   coe.int/echr/Homepage_EN (accessed 15 February 2009).

5 See the Immigration Act 1971 and the British Nationality Act 1981, both available via www.england-legislation.hmso.gov.uk/revisedstatutes/uk-acts-1981a (accessed 9 July 2009).

6 See the full text of this speech at www.guardian.co.uk/politics/2004/apr/27/ immigrationpolicy.speeches (accessed 9 July 2009).

7 www.amnesty.org.uk/uploads/documents/doc_16178.pdf (accessed 16 February 2009).

8 The slogan comes from the title of a 2003 Green Paper of the same name, and is the name of a Government programme for children and young people, with a website at www.dcsf.gov.uk/everychildmatters/ (accessed 9 July 2009).

9 H. Crawley and T. Lester, 'No place for a child: children in UK immigration detention – impacts, alternatives and safeguards' (Save the Children, 2005).

10 European Court of Human Rights, Application number 13229/03 (2008), available via the ECHR HUDOC database at www.echr.coe.int/ECHR/EN/Header/Case-Law/ HUDOC/HUDOC+database/ (accessed 16 February 2009).

2a Roger Zetter

Curtailing freedoms, diminishing rights in Britain's asylum policy: a narrative of 'them' and 'us'

Immigration and asylum policies ask crucial questions about national identity, about human rights, and about our values as compassionate citizens in an era of increasingly complex international challenges. Yet, except for small numbers of academics, advocates and activists, there is diminishing public concern for the way in which the increasingly draconian British asylum and immigration policies of the last fifteen years have become normalised into our national way of life, legislation and values. Public discourse and popular rhetoric increasingly legitimise the diminution of rights to which asylum seekers are entitled, and the depletion of the state's moral obligations enshrined in the 1951 *Convention Relating to the Status of Refugees* (the Geneva Convention).

Shami Chakrabarti challenges this state of affairs. It is a privilege to reflect on the significance of her contribution to the debate and to consider some of the contextual issues and questions which her essay raises.

Setting the context

A new era of international migration, and in particular the increasingly global search for asylum, has had profound impacts on the political landscape of the United Kingdom. Chakrabarti's essay provides an eloquently powerful reminder that those disturbing features of this new landscape, the incarceration and arbitrary detention of asylum seekers, are not just the instruments of faraway, repressive governments: they are increasingly embedded in the fabric of a liberal democratic state like Britain.

These instruments form the apex of a new apparatus of state power intended to deter some of the world's most vulnerable people from seeking asylum, and to restrict the rights and life chances of those who do manage to gain entry to Britain. Defining the main contours of this apparatus are: at least six major new statutes since 1993 dealing with asylum and immigration; major new institutional structures (such as the National Asylum Support Service, and the Border and Immigration Agency[1]); new policy initiatives such as the compulsory dispersal of asylum seekers to deprived inner city locations; procedures such as the New Asylum Model introduced in 2006 to fast-track asylum claims; the gradual withdrawal of asylum seeker rights of appeal and representation; and the growing list of so-called 'safe countries'.

Despite the fact that asylum claims have declined from a peak of over one hundred thousand per annum in 2002 to less than twenty-five thousand per annum in 2007, refusal rates are as high as ever, while removal and interdiction practices have been extended, notably family removal, alongside increasing controls on unaccompanied children seeking asylum. Estimates suggest that the UK asylum system costs about £1.5 billion per annum to run, which is almost twice the annual budget of the international refugee agency the Office of the United Nations High Commissioner for Refugees (UNHCR). Nor should we forget the wider context of European Union harmonisation of asylum and immigration policy and practice, agreed in the Treaty of Amsterdam in 1997.[2] Deterrence and restrictionism towards asylum seekers are the cornerstones of an emerging Europe-wide policy of 'managed migration' in order to combat the global phenomenon of the 'asylum-migration nexus'[3] and the ethnic 'super-diversity' of migrants arriving in the global north.[4] However, with the possible exception of France and the Netherlands, in no European country but Britain has the issue of immigration and immigration control encompassed such an enduringly problematic political and social agenda.

In short, with increasingly muted public protest, Britain remains at the forefront of countries adopting a hard line stance on asylum, despite being one of the original thirteen signatories of the 1951 Geneva Convention.

How can we account for this state of affairs and what are the consequences? In order to answer, it is necessary to consider an underlying, more profound set of issues concerned with the circumstances under which, and the ways in which, a state should identify and protect its interests. In the context of asylum and immigration these questions speak to a narrative about 'them' and 'us', because the relentless deprivation of 'their' rights and liberties sits alongside the gradual diminution and loss of 'our' rights as well, and our co-optation into the declining moral obligations and humanitarian values of a liberal democratic state.

'Them' . . .

Many factors underpin the contemporary political concerns and highlight significant issues in the social relations between 'us' and 'them'.[5]

The increasing volume of migrants, and particularly the rapid rise in asylum seeking until 2002, has challenged the Government's intention to manage these inflows in an environment marked by increasingly hostile race relations.[6] These concerns were underscored by the growing ethnic, religious and cultural diversity of asylum seekers and migrants more generally, which confronted perceptions of a cohesive 'national identity' and long-standing assumptions about the norms of British citizenship. The backcloth of so-called global terrorism, and the 'securitisation of migration', has heightened these anxieties about the 'other', about who belongs and thus who we are. Since the majority of asylum seekers come from Islamic countries, which are also labelled as the source of global terrorism, eliding asylum seekers with a threat to national security has been a popular though entirely false discourse.

Thus migrants, and especially asylum seekers and refugees who have been allowed to settle, were problematised, in policy terms, around a perception that they somehow challenged notions of a cohesive 'national identity'. Accordingly, citizenship and community cohesion policies have become both a panacea for dealing with 'them' and a tool kit to replace multi-culturalism (a failing policy in the Government's eyes) with a much stronger assimilationist form of migrant incorporation. A reassuring vocabulary of cohesion diminishes the perceived threats of diversity and resonates with a government dominated by security fears.

Moreover, although the 'new migration' reflects complex global processes and a diverse demographic structure, it is asylum seekers who have been targeted as the principal focus of Britain's immigration policies since the early 1990s. Government policies which deterred and restricted entry of asylum seekers, yet simultaneously promoted cohesion and assimilation of migrant communities, gave contradictory and conflicting messages. Controversial legislative changes since 1993 centralised control of welfare provision for asylum seekers. But this undermined, rather than supported, the capacity of service agencies to provide for these welfare needs, while dispersal intensified host population resentment about access to housing and other public resources in locations already experiencing high levels of social deprivation.[7] Ambiguous and often hostile and strident media messages fuelled these anxieties about public services and national 'identity'.

Singled out by legislation and policy, and further marginalised by their temporary immigration status, asylum seekers became, at least in the public mind, a proxy and a convenient shorthand for all the perceived problems attributed to the 'new migration'. The label 'asylum seeker' was formed, transformed and politicised by this conjuncture of government policies and public rhetoric. Thus the label, and the identity it purported to convey, reproduced itself in the prevailing political discourse and in a popular vocabulary, which has been instrumental in further reinforcing the image of 'them' as the 'other':

> 'spontaneous asylum seekers' (with implications of fecklessness and presumably different from a planned asylum seeker), 'illegal asylum seekers', 'bogus asylum seekers', 'economic refugee/asylum seeker', 'illegal migrant', 'trafficked migrant', 'over-stayers', 'failed asylum seeker' (note not failed refugee), 'undocumented asylum seeker/migrant'. The vocabulary is varied in its scope but singular in its covert

intention – to convey an image of marginality, dishonesty, a threat, unwelcomed, the 'wasted lives' of Bauman's vividly titled book (2004).[8]

The Government's deterrence policies and practices, reproduced in a popular and pejorative discourse, subvert the true meaning of the label 'asylum seeker', curtail previously enjoyed rights, and, at the extreme, criminalise those desperately seeking asylum. The ironic outcome is a new set of labels which compound the perception that the protective labels 'asylum seeker' and 'refugee' are no longer a basic Geneva Convention right, but a highly privileged prize which few deserve and most claim illegally. As the UK Government, and indeed many European Union partners, increasingly try to force asylum seekers into the mould of irregular migration, pre-empt arrival and contain them in regions of origin or 'safe third countries', the exceptional status of refugees within the context of immigration is now in doubt. The 1951 Convention inscribed the right to claim asylum in a country of choice, at a time of choice and without penalty. In all these respects this right is now heavily circumscribed. What was originally a convention to protect people whose lives were in danger and a tool of empowerment against state power, is increasingly and ironically being turned on its head by national legislation, policies and practices to become an instrument to persecute the persecuted. Seeking asylum is no longer a right and last resort but reconstructed as a highly constrained privilege.

... and 'us'

At the same time, the present state of affairs invokes a (perhaps disturbing) narrative about 'us' and our response to the 'other'. There are two arguments here: one pertaining to the loss of rights, the other to the diminution of humanitarian and moral obligations.

In a 2007 report, evocatively titled 'Prisoners of terrorism: the impact of anti-terrorism measures on refugees and asylum seekers in Britain', the Refugee Council highlighted the impact of the securitisation of migration. But we may equally ask about the impact of anti-terrorism measures on 'us', because the loss of asylum seeker rights is mirrored in our own loss of rights, which has been portrayed as necessary to protect our own security. The price we have paid is substantial.

Chakrabarti's essay explores in detail one element of this: the way in which detention of asylum seekers and others, without trial, diminishes not just the rights of those who are detained but the rights of us all. Exactly the same conclusion applies to the introduction of national identity cards and the fingerprinting of asylum seekers. Both these policies have been justified on exactly the same grounds: the need to contain the perceived threat to security which migrants are thought to pose. And, as I have argued, asylum seekers are stereotyped in this context as the proxy for the much broader and more complex transnational processes of migration. Setting aside the, at least questionable, linkage of national security to migration (since the migration component is a relatively small element in the geopolitics of international terrorism), the bigger issue is that of trust between the state and its citizens. ID cards and fingerprinting represent significant developments in the surveillance society, developments which tilt the balance of power firmly towards the state, and reduce the rights and the liberties of the individual.

Similarly, prosecution for glorifying terrorism, even given the dubious possibility of legal proof, undermines freedom of speech and impacts on us all, not just on asylum seekers and other migrants. In any case, there are important distinctions between terrorism, freedom fighters and resistance. Ironically, of course, asylum seekers are precisely those whose actions of fleeing persecutory, violent and frequently terrorising regimes, speak out against regimes whose abuse of human rights we deplore. But all our freedoms are diminished by this control of freedom of speech and the increasing surveillance of our identity and lives.

The restructuring of the Immigration and Nationality Department, deemed unfit for purpose by a former Home Secretary, reinforces these concerns.[9] In this context, the change to the Border and Immigration Agency was not just a bureaucratic reorganisation with a functional title, but a conjuncture of words conveying highly politicised messages about the identity of Britain as nation state, defined in terms of territory and membership, with boundaries protected as much for whom they exclude as for whom they contain.

In short, an almost automatic link between terrorism and asylum claimants – the 'securitisation of asylum and immigration' – not only drives legislation which denies the rights of the asylum seeker minority itself, but also adds to the wider sense of a political environment increasingly dominated by a persecutory disposition which undermines all our freedoms.

However, from another perspective, the response to asylum seekers, and migrants more generally, has brought about a more profound loss: the loss of moral obligations expected in a liberal democratic state. This loss permeates many aspects of the political discourse and social relations in contemporary Britain. What began as an invited migration of dissidents and refugees in the nineteenth century and then became a humanitarian obligation in the twentieth century under the 1951 Convention, has been transformed into an issue of nationality, sovereignty, belonging and exclusion of those who most need the protection of their basic rights. Asylum seekers have become stereotyped by a rhetoric of regulatory exclusion which compounds a sense of otherness and a status, not as a protected minority, but as those whose presence is perceived to reinforce socio-economic and cultural concerns about how we live in a multi-cultural society. These concerns have been channelled into immigration discourse in general and the asylum discourse in particular. Asylum seekers are an easy target on which to focus a range of concerns about collective identity and anti-immigration rhetoric.

The complex array of asylum and immigration legislation is the vehicle for mediating these state interests. But institutionalising public disquiet in a complex array of democratically accepted legislation has a malign effect: it legitimises the political objective that seeks to present the regulating of claims as no more than a natural and depoliticised bureaucratic process, rather than a profoundly important humanitarian obligation to support a potentially life and death decision for asylum claimants. A 2006 communication by the UNHCR highlights precisely this danger of confusing the inviolable right of protection for refugees with the objective of national border protection in order to manage other patterns and processes of migration.[10]

More than this, it is not only the Government, acting in the name of the state, which widens its powers in our name and reproduces social concerns about immigration as normal policy and practice. Fines for employers using asylum seekers debarred from work, carriers' liability, and criminalising so-called 'illegal entry' all exemplify the statutory provisions which extend the state's reach beyond its own agency to co-opt us all in this enterprise. Incorporating the wider community as agents of national immigration policies, at the same time as criminalising our non-compliance, such measures further legitimise state agency in controlling immigration.[11]

But illegality is a constructed concept, not an a priori or objective condition. Asylum seekers and those who employ them 'illegally' are not increasingly criminal *per se*, but only so in terms of a state seeking to define who belongs and to exclude who does not. The fact that asylum seekers are so active and persistent in trying to claim their rights does not negate their claim. Ironically the threat of death may be as great in seeking entry as it is in leaving a country where one was persecuted or caught up in conflict. But criminalising this process of seeking asylum is a denial of rights and a denial of a moral obligation of the receiving state. We want asylum seekers to be constructed as stereotypical victims, but when they do not conform to this stereotype, or when they arrive 'illegally', we designate them opportunists with no call on our moral obligations.

Borders are thus privileged over humanitarian needs and obligations. But the situation I outline here transcends the institutional and statutory processes of immigration and asylum law in Britain. It speaks to anxieties about the 'other', and about social relations between asylum seekers and what it means to be British. It speaks to a growing preoccupation, not just in Britain, in which apparently secure 'identities' and 'nationalisms' diminish in an era of global migration. Asylum seekers are a potent representation of these concerns.

Conclusion

Shami Chakrabarti's essay on detention of asylum seekers opens a window not just on the rights of asylum claimants, but on our own social world, and on our rights and obligations as citizens in a liberal democratic society. We need a political rhetoric which educates and transforms public attitudes, not in ways which distrust asylum seekers and refugees, but which assert the protection of all our human rights and humanitarian obligations. Focusing in detail on just one aspect of this complex, diffuse and often contradictory arena of asylum and immigration law, Chakrabarti's essay is a powerful contribution to this much-needed rhetoric.

Notes

1 Editor's note: in March 2008 the Border and Immigration Agency was reformed into the UK Border Agency. Roger Zetter's text was written in October 2007.
2 R. Zetter, D. Griffiths, N. Sigona and S. Ferretti, 'An assessment of the impact of asylum policies in Europe 1990–2000', a report of a study commissioned by the Home Office Research Development and Statistics Directorate, Social and Economic Research Publications Series, Research Study 259 (London: 2003), www.homeoffice.gov.uk/rds/pdfs2/hors259.pdf (accessed 20 February 2009); A. Geddes, *The Politics of Migration and Immigration in Europe* (London, Thousand Oaks, New Delhi: Sage, 2003); C. Boswell, *European Migration Policies in Flux: Changing Patterns of Inclusion and Exclusion* (London: Royal Institute of International Affairs, Blackwell, 2003).
3 S. Castles, 'Towards a sociology of forced migration and transformation', *Sociology* 37:1 (2003).
4 S. Vertovec, 'The emergence of super-diversity in Britain', University of Oxford, the Centre on Migration, Policy and Society (COMPAS) Working Paper WP-06-25 (Oxford: 2006).
5 R. Zetter, D. Griffiths and N. Sigona, 'Social capital or social exclusion? The impact of asylum seeker dispersal on refugee community based organisations', *Community Development Journal* 40:2 (2005).
6 T. Cantle, *Community Cohesion: A New Framework for Race and Diversity* (Basingstoke: Palgrave/Macmillan 2005).
7 Zetter *et al.*, 'Social capital or social exclusion?'; see note 5.
8 R. Zetter, 'More labels, fewer refugees: making and remaking the refugee label in an era of globalisation', *Journal of Refugee Studies* 20:2 (2007); Z. Bauman, *Wasted Lives: Modernity and its Outcasts* (Cambridge: Polity Press, 2004).
9 http://news.bbc.co.uk/1/hi/uk_politics/5007148.stm (accessed 20 February 2009).
10 The Office of the United Nations High Commissioner for Refugees, *The State of the World's Refugees: Human Displacement in the New Millennium* (Oxford: Oxford University Press, 2006).
11 To paraphrase Zetter, 'More labels, fewer refugees'; see note 8.

3 Lawrence O. Gostin

'Old' and 'new' institutions for persons with mental illness: treatment, punishment, or preventive confinement?[1]

In 1972, I covertly entered a brutal, inhumane institution for the criminally insane in eastern North Carolina as a pseudo-patient under a US Department of Justice study. What I experienced during those many weeks would shape how I view what Erving Goffman called 'total institutions'.[2] Since that formative experience as a young law student I have closely observed institutions that warehouse persons with mental illness in many regions of the world ranging from the Americas and Europe to the Indian subcontinent and Asia. Those experiences, together with the careful study of human rights reports and judicial decisions, have led me to one simple conclusion. Despite countless promises for a better life by national commissions, governments, and the international community, there has evolved a vicious cycle of neglect, abandonment, indignity, cruel and inhumane treatment, and punishment of persons with mental illness. This is not true in every place, time, and circumstance; there are pockets of deep caring and compassion. But for the vast majority, and in most geographic regions, this sad fact remains a tragic reality.

The shameful history of benign, and sometimes malignant, neglect of persons with mental illness is well understood: the deep stigma and unredressed discrimination, the deplorable living conditions, and the physical and social barriers preventing their integration and full participation in society. The maltreatment of this vulnerable population has been reinforced by the hurtful stereotypes of incompetency and dangerousness.

A person's competency is his or her most valuable attribute. If the public perceives, or if a court determines, that a person is incompetent, it robs him or her of all dignity, including the right to control the most fundamental aspects of life such as bodily integrity and personal or financial affairs. Most persons with mental illness are, in contrast, competent to make decisions about their lives. They may lack competency to perform certain tasks at particular times, but rarely are they generally incompetent, as is often assumed in law and practice.

The belief that persons with mental illness are uniformly dangerous is an equally harmful myth. It provides policy makers with an ostensible justification to exercise control over people with mental illness even if they have not committed a violent offence. Yet research demonstrates that the class of people with mental illness is no more dangerous than other populations.[3]

In this essay I will show how this vulnerable population has been unconscionably treated. First, I will examine the gross human rights violations that have occurred, and continue to occur, in what I am calling 'old' psychiatric institutions. During the second half of the twentieth century, however, many of these old institutions were closed as part of a social compact with mentally ill persons and their families to provide community care. The deinstitutionalisation movement, however, resulted in new places of confinement for this population: jails, prisons, and homeless shelters. In the second part of this essay, I will explore the new realities of criminal confinement of persons with mental illness. As we will see, incarceration of this vulnerable population in the criminal justice system has caused enormous suffering. And, if the assertion, attributed to Dostoyevsky, that 'the degree of civilization . . . can be judged by entering its prisons' is correct, then by that measure we are a deeply uncivilised society.

Psychiatric hospitals: the continuing legacy of neglect and abuse

Persons with mental illness seek four interrelated human rights: freedom from unwarranted detention (liberty), humane living conditions (dignity), amelioration of stigma and discrimination (equality), and access to high quality mental health services (entitlement).[4] These principles are enshrined in international law in treaties and declarations that directly apply to the rights of persons with mental illness. In 1991, the United Nations adopted *Principles for the Protection of Persons with Mental Illness and for the Improvement of Mental Health Care* (the MI Principles).[5] The MI Principles include a preference for community care; the right to the least restrictive environment; clear standards and natural justice for compulsory admission; legal representation; and the right to information.

In 2006, the United Nations adopted the *Convention on the Rights of Persons with Disabilities*.[6] Article 1 specifically includes persons with mental impairments, 'which in interaction with various barriers may hinder their full and effective participation in society on an equal basis with others'. Article 15 prohibits torture or cruel, inhuman or degrading treatment or punishment; Article 22 protects the right to privacy and health information; Article 25 grants equal access to the highest attainable standard of care, without discrimination; and Article 29 guarantees the equal right to participate in political life.[7]

Finally, the World Health Organization (WHO) runs projects on the human rights of people with mental disabilities. The WHO's work has multiple themes, including the right to the highest attainable standard of mental healthcare; freedom from physical, sexual and mental abuse and other forms of inhuman and degrading treatment; the right to liberty, autonomy and security of the person; the right to equality, dignity and respect; and the right to be free from discrimination in the exercise of political, civil, religious, social and cultural rights.

These themes correspond to the human rights principles of liberty, dignity, equality and entitlement that I have suggested above. And they are the focus of a strand of human rights jurisprudence that exists principally in Europe, but which in the early twenty-first century is now emerging in the Americas. I will now discuss some cases that have a bearing on these four themes; they involve involuntary detention, conditions of confinement, civil rights, and mental health services.[8]

Liberty: involuntary confinement

Article 5 of the *European Convention on Human Rights* guarantees the right to liberty and security of the person.[9] The 1979 case of *Winterwerp v. the Netherlands* established that civil commitment must follow a 'procedure prescribed by law' and cannot be arbitrary; the person must have a recognised mental illness, and require confinement for the purposes of treatment: 'Except in emergency cases, the individual concerned should not be deprived of his liberty unless he has been reliably shown to be of "unsound mind". The very nature of what has to be established before the competent national authority – that is a true mental disorder – calls for objective medical expertise.'

Furthermore, the 1981 case of *X v. the United Kingdom*, which I brought while Legal Director of MIND (the National Association for Mental Health, in the United Kingdom), mandated speedy periodic review by a court with the essential elements of due process. *Habeas corpus* was insufficient for these purposes because it simply reviewed the technical lawfulness of the detention, but not the substantive justification.

Following the trend of these two cases, the European Court of Human Rights (ECHR) has been highly active in addressing the human rights of persons with mental illness under Article 5 of the European Convention, requiring a recognised mental illness and a speedy independent hearing by a court for involuntary admission to hospital. But what if a person is 'voluntarily' admitted, but in fact has not given consent? The problem of 'non-protesting' patients arises when persons are confined in fact but not under the force of law. A person may succumb to a show of authority or may be unable to provide consent. In Britain in the 1998 *Bournewood* ruling,[10] the House of Lords ruled that an informal patient incapable of giving consent was not 'detained' and even if he were, there was common law power to restrain and detain a mentally incapacitated person in his best interests.

In *HL v. the United Kingdom* in 2004, however, the ECHR held that parts of Article 5 of the European Convention had been breached in *Bournewood*: 'The right to liberty in a democratic society is too important for a person to lose the benefit of Convention protection simply because they have given themselves up to detention, especially when they are not capable of consenting to, or disagreeing with, the proposed action.'[11]

Dignity: conditions of confinement

Non-governmental organisations continue to find appalling conditions in institutions and residential homes for persons with mental illness. These include long periods of isolation in filthy, closed spaces; lack of care and medical treatment such as failure to provide nursing and mental health services as well as essential medicines; and severe maltreatment such as being beaten, tied up, and denied basic nutrition and clothing. Dealing with the *Herczegfalvy* v. *Austria* case in 1992, the ECHR said that vigilance is vital due to 'the position of powerlessness which is typical of patients confined in psychiatric hospitals'. This case involved a patient who was unnecessarily and involuntarily sedated and tied to a hospital bed for several weeks. Despite the profession of vigilance, the ECHR found no violation of Article 3 of the European Convention, forbidding torture and inhuman or degrading treatment or punishment, because the action was 'therapeutically necessary'. But how could such maltreatment be either therapeutic or necessary?

Two cases which I brought while at MIND illustrate the extent to which European jurisprudence during the 1980s was highly deferential to medical opinion in cases involving inhuman and degrading treatment; more so than in the handling of Article 5 cases involving the right to liberty. In one case, the European Commission found no violation of Article 3.[12] A patient in Broadmoor high-security psychiatric hospital was kept in a ward with beds inches apart, with no safety or security, and he had not seen a doctor for nearly ten years. In the second, I was asked by the Commission to visit a man in Broadmoor who had been placed in isolation. He had been in a tiny cell for five weeks. I was told that he was extremely dangerous. However, when I entered the cell, he was sitting naked, huddled in a corner. The smell of the room was so putrid, caked with excrement and soaked in urine, that I was overpowered and had to leave. The patient had been allowed out only for twenty minutes per day. The Commission forced a 'friendly settlement', under which the patient was paid a paltry sum.

More recently, the Court has required increased medical attention and appropriate facilities for persons with mental illness. More importantly, it has emphasised that the European Convention's proscription of inhuman and degrading treatment includes actions designed to humiliate persons with mental illness.

Beyond Europe, a new generation of impassioned advocates is bringing cases to the Inter-American Commission on Human Rights (IACHR) with promising results.[13] In the 1999 case of *Victor Rosario Congo* v. *Ecuador*, the IACHR found a violation of the right to humane treatment. A person with mental illness had been struck in the head, denied medical treatment, and left in his cell for forty days. The case is important because the IACHR relied on the above-mentioned United Nations *Principles for the Protection of Persons with Mental Illness*, interpreting inhuman and degrading treatment or punishment so as to extend the widest possible protection against abuses, whether physical or mental. The IACHR asserted that 'a violation of the right to physical integrity is even more serious in the case of a person held in preventive detention, suffering a mental disease, and therefore in the custody of the State in a particularly vulnerable position'.[14]

In addition, the IACHR *Rules of Procedure* allow 'precautionary measures' to be taken 'in serious and urgent cases . . . to prevent irreparable harm to persons'.[15] In December 2003, for the first time in its forty-four-year history, the IACHR approved 'precautionary measures' to protect the lives, liberty, and personal security of 460 people detained in a psychiatric institution in Paraguay. Two boys, who were the focus of the case, had been in isolation for more than four years, naked, and without access to bathrooms. They were held in bare cells with holes in the floor that should have functioned as latrines but were caked over with excrement. They spent approximately four hours of every other day in an outdoor pen littered with human excrement, garbage, and broken glass. The precautionary measures adopted by the IACHR require Paraguay to protect the lives and physical and mental safety of the 460 people detained in the institution, as well as to comply with international protocols on the use of isolation. By using 'precautionary measures', advocates can avoid the burdensome and time-consuming process of 'exhausting domestic remedies' before gaining access to the IACHR. The 'precautionary measures' procedure, therefore, promises to help redress the countless cases of maltreatment and abuse of persons with mental illness in the Americas.

The maltreatment of persons with mental illness is an international problem, well beyond Europe and the Americas.[16] During an investigation of Japanese mental hospitals, I found abysmal conditions.[17] In one hospital a patient had been secluded for some thirty years. The conditions in which he lived were so restricted that he had lost the use of his legs. Adjacent to his cell was a large cavern in the floor where dozens of patients were placed and bathed at the same time. Yet, in India I found that many of the hospitals were not crowded and the conditions amiable.

What was the reason for the differences between Japan and India? In Japan, mental illness was a shame, and families would shun those with supposed abnormalities. But in India, the culture was to care for mentally ill persons within their families and communities. It is clear that cultural acceptance of mental illness as part of the human condition is a powerful predictor of how well people will be treated and integrated into society.

Equality: civil rights

Human rights norms extend to the exercise of a wide array of civil rights both within and outside institutions. Simply because a person has a mental illness, or is subject to confinement, does not mean he or she is incapable of exercising the rights of citizenship. Human rights bodies have helped secure equality through norms of access to the courts and privacy. The ECHR has found violations of the right to a fair and public hearing in the determination of a person's civil rights. The subject matter of these cases includes the right to control property, to exercise parental rights, and to be granted a hearing in the determination of incompetency or placement into guardianship.[18]

The right to a 'private and family life' under the *European Convention on Human Rights* can be a powerful tool to safeguard the civil rights of persons with mental illness. The ECHR, for example, has applied this privacy protection to free correspondence, informational privacy, marriage, and the parent-child relationship.[19] It has, thus far, declined to do so for sexual freedoms, but advocates are pursuing cases to defend this form of intimacy.

Entitlement: the right to mental health services

The final human rights theme of entitlement is more fragile than the others, involving the right of access to core mental health services. Although essential health services have a basis in ethics, they are more difficult to attain under international law. The right to health is a social and economic entitlement. Notably the European Convention does not capture this set of entitlements. The IACHR also has not pursued the right to health even though the *Protocol of San Salvador* enunciates a full set of health rights.[20] Consequently, the scope and definition of the right to mental health has remained vague and variable.

But several contemporary initiatives on health rights in general and mental health rights in particular are promising. In 2000 the United Nations Committee on Economic, Social and Cultural Rights issued General Comment 14 on the Right to Health.[21] The UN Commission on Human Rights subsequently appointed a Special Rapporteur with a mandate to focus on the right to health.[22] The Rapporteur's first report in 2003 identified three primary objectives: to promote the right to health as a fundamental human right; to clarify its contours; and to identify good practices for operationalising the right.[23] The Rapporteur subsequently published a report in 2005 on the right to health for persons with mental illness, which offers a comprehensive account of the elements to adequate mental health services.[24]

Also at this global scale, the World Health Organization has a project focusing on mental health and human rights.[25] One part of this project is a mental health legislation manual that provides a tool for countries to adopt international human rights norms into domestic legislation.[26] One key such norm is the provision of 'public mental health', which frames the right to mental health in terms of population-based services. Thus, countries would be responsible for offering screening for mental illnesses, mental health education, and psychiatric services in hospitals and the community. These, then, are some of the ways in which jurisprudence is striving to improve the rights of persons with mental illness. But international human rights norms will have maximum impact only if they are adopted by nations into domestic laws, policies and programmes.

The transmigration from 'old' to 'new' institutions: the moral outrage of the mentally ill in prison

During the mid-twentieth century, health services for seriously mentally ill individuals were almost exclusively provided in large, often Victorian, institutions. Since that time, there has been wide recognition that psychiatric institutions are unacceptable places to care for and treat persons with mental illness: they are prohibitively costly, isolating and neglectful, and sometimes abusive and punitive. In the USA, civil rights advocates in the 1960s, in an unlikely alliance with fiscal conservatives, fought to close these institutions. These activists believed that persons with mental illness have rights and should be integrated in the community. They reformed mental health laws to establish more rigorous standards and procedures for compulsory admission, and litigated to close antiquated institutions. Around the same time, fiscal conservatives felt that psychiatric institutions were too expensive. For example, Ronald Reagan, then Governor of California, began the dismantling of state mental hospitals.

Known as deinstitutionalisation, the unequivocal promise made to persons with mental illness and their families was that the state would erect a social safety net in the community, including supportive housing and mental health services. That promise, possibly fraudulent at inception, was never kept. Community mental health services were chronically underfunded, fragmented, and often punitive.[27] At the same time, the public clamoured to remove the mentally ill from their neighbourhoods, a call that resonated well with 'law and order' politicians. These public feelings were inflamed by press reports of violence by a minute percentage of persons with mental illness, as well as by the spectre of homeless people on their streets.

What transpired was a massive transmigration of mentally ill people from 'old' to 'new' institutions: jails, remand centres, prisons, nursing homes, and homeless shelters. Many people with mental illness were simply left destitute on the streets. We pass them every day in urban areas as we avert our eyes and step over or around them. Most of the mentally ill languishing in the streets or the correctional system are poor, and often from racial or ethnic minorities. The correctional system has become the mental health system of last resort, as this population has been segregated and forgotten. Incarceration and homelessness have become part of life for society's most vulnerable population.

It did not have to be that way. There are good data to show that mental institutions can close in ways that are beneficial to patients if there are adequate discharge planning and community services.[28] What is needed is the political will to provide a range of supportive and psychiatric services in the community. But that never happened for the vast majority of persons with mental illness.

Incarceration of the mentally ill

The data on incarceration of persons with mental illness are not fully collected in many parts of the world, and there are surely differences among the various countries and regions. Nevertheless, the data that do exist paint a picture of vast numbers of seriously mentally ill people in the correctional system. Prevalence rates for all forms of mental illness in the prison population are markedly higher than rates in the community.[29] In many different countries, severe mental illness occurs five to ten times more frequently among people in prison than in the general population.[30] These data hold true in countries as diverse as Australia,[31] Iran,[32] New Zealand,[33] the United Kingdom,[34] and the United States.[35]

Mentally ill prisoners, moreover, are highly vulnerable. This population is twice as likely to have been homeless before entering prison. They suffer disproportionately from co-morbidities with drug and alcohol abuse. While in prison, few inmates receive access to adequate mental health services – both psychological care and essential medicines. Mentally ill prisoners are at very high risk of harm or death. Many experience physical or sexual abuse and are injured before and during their time in confinement. One study found mentally ill prisoners were seventeen times more likely than the general population to die within two weeks following release.[36]

Prisons as toxic, non-therapeutic environments

Most of the mentally ill who are incarcerated begin in jails or remand centres pending trial. There is usually no professional screening for mental illness, and there are few methods of diversion from the criminal justice system. Some are so actively psychotic (e.g. schizophrenic or manic depressive) that any layperson would notice: they might be hearing voices, talking to God, withdrawn, incoherently mumbling, displaying dissociation from social life, playing with excrement, and self-mutilating. Others have a variety of clinical symptoms that require professional mental health treatment. These men and women then find themselves in prisons that are overwhelmed by numbers and by the impossibility of providing humane, effective mental health services in punitive institutions. In many prison systems, only a small fraction have access to mental health treatment. Many more suffer from poor diagnosis, lack of timely access, an over-belief that prisoners are 'just faking', over-sedation as a form of behaviour control, and an inadequate control of side effects that might include uncontrollable shaking, obesity and diabetes, or heat reactions. Many prison systems offer, at best, crisis management for the mentally ill.

Even if prisons could offer decent mental health services, they are counter-therapeutic, toxic environments. Mentally ill inmates, at the extreme, may have little appreciation of why or how they were imprisoned. They may have serious difficulties in cognition, emotion, interpersonal skills, and impulse control. Mentally ill prisoners are often subjects of derision, abuse and violence by other inmates and correctional staff. They are unable to fend off sexual and other violent assaults. More importantly, prison philosophy is infused with keeping rules and discipline, and severely punishing those who fail to comply or simply are disruptive. Consequently, mentally ill prisoners find themselves in segregated, high security settings or, worse, in seclusion. Their conditions of confinement can be much worse, even, than those of the general prison population. And, they are unable to cope with the loneliness, harshness and pain inflicted in these settings. They deteriorate mentally, repeatedly break rules, re-enter isolation, and have their sentences extended – an endless, vicious cycle of inhuman and degrading treatment.

Inhuman and degrading treatment in the correctional system
Human rights activists who so deplored the conditions of 'old' psychiatric hospitals, and fought so hard for their closure would be dismayed to observe the same kinds of abusive conditions in prisons. Just as human rights bodies found that mental hospital conditions violated international law, so too have they made the same findings in prisons.

In some cases, the ECHR has been as timid as it was in the early mental hospital cases. For example, in *Kudla* v. *Poland* in 2002, the Court found no violation of Article 3, despite the fact that an inmate received no mental health services during three years of pre-trial detention: 'The Court has consistently stressed that the suffering and humiliation involved must in any event go beyond that inevitable element of suffering or humiliation connected with a given form of legitimate treatment or punishment.' But how is the absence of services for a person with mental illness legitimate, and why should the mentally ill be punished for years even before a trial?

The Court in other cases, however, has condemned harsh prison conditions. It has found a violation of Article 3 in cases where prisoners were segregated and had their sentences extended, thereby threatening a mentally ill inmate's 'physical and moral resistance'; this was 'not compatible with the standard of treatment required in respect of a mentally ill person'. Similarly, it has criticised abhorrent conditions in detention centres, including overcrowded and dirty cells with insufficient sanitary and sleeping facilities, insufficient hot water, no fresh air or daylight, and no exercise facilities. Although there was no deliberate ill-treatment, the conditions alone were so awful that they violated Article 3. In a direct repudiation of its earlier statements regarding mental hospitals, the Court found, in *Dougoz* v. *Greece* in 2005, that an Article 3 violation could be found if the cumulative effects of the conditions were sufficiently abhorrent.

Even the conditions in psychiatric wings of prisons have been found to be inhuman and degrading. In *Peers* v. *Greece* in 2001, the Court found an Article 3 violation when prisoners were detained in very small cells, the toilets were not screened, there was no adequate ventilation, and it was extremely hot. Although there was no intention to humiliate or debase the prisoners, the conditions in which they lived caused feelings of anguish and inferiority capable of humiliating and debasing them.

Promises made and breached: from neglect to abuse and punishment

Governments and civil society, in all parts of the world, have treated persons with mental illness horribly in old and new institutions. Countless promises have been made to right the wrongs, but these promises were dishonoured in practice. Instead of a future of compassion, care and integration in the community, the mentally ill have experienced a perpetual cycle of coercion and maltreatment. Perhaps it is time to see this issue not so much as a social problem, but as a human rights imperative, one which we must follow by adopting the principles of liberty, dignity, equality and entitlement.

Notes

1   I thank John Kraemer, an extraordinarily capable Georgetown law student, for research on this text.
2   E. Goffman, *Asylums: Essays on the Condition of the Social Situation of Mental Patients and Other Inmates* (New York: Doubleday, 1961).
3   S. Fazel and M. Grann, 'The population impact of severe mental illness on violent crime', *American Journal of Psychiatry* 163 (2006).
4   R. J. Bonnie, 'Three strands of mental health law: developmental mileposts', in L. E. Frost and R. J. Bonnie (eds), *The Evolution of Mental Health Law* (Washington, DC: American Psychology Association, 2001).
5   For the full principles, see www.unhchr.ch/html/menu3/b/68.htm (accessed 12 February 2009).
6   Available at www.un.org/disabilities/default.asp?id=259 (accessed 12 February 2009).
7   For discussion, see M. Jones, 'Can international law improve mental health? Some thoughts on the proposed convention on the rights of people with disabilities', *International Journal of Law and Psychiatry* 28:2 (2005).
8   For a detailed examination of mental health and human rights jurisprudence, see L. O. Gostin and L. Gable, 'The human rights of persons with mental illness: a global perspective on the application of human rights principles to mental health', *Maryland Law Review* 63 (2004); B. Hale, 'Justice and equality in mental health law: the European experience', *International Journal of Law and Psychiatry* 30:1 (2007).

9   The *European Convention on Human Rights* can be read via www.echr.coe.int, where one can also find judgments of the European Court of Human Rights (ECHR) via the HUDOC online database (accessed 12 February 2009).

10 *R. v. Bournewood Community and Mental Health NHS Trust, ex parte L*, [1998] 3 All ER 289.

11 See P. Fennell, 'Convention compliance: public safety, and the social inclusion of mentally disordered people', *Journal of Law and Society* 32:1 (2005).

12 Until 1998, individuals could not apply directly to the ECHR but had to apply via the European Commission of Human Rights, which could then address the matter with the ECHR.

13 See L. Gable, J. Vasquez, L. O. Gostin and H. V. Jimenez, 'Mental health and human rights in the Americas: protecting the human rights of persons involuntarily admitted to and detained in psychiatric institutions', *Pan American Journal of Public Health* 18:4–5 (2005).

14 Case 11.427, Inter-American Court of Human Rights 63/99, paragraph 67 (1999), available at www.cidh.oas.org/annualrep/98eng/merits/Ecuador%2011427.htm. (accessed 15 February 2009).

15 *Rules of Procedure of the Inter-American Court of Human Rights* (Approved by the Commission at its 109th special session held from 4 to 8 December 2000 and amended at its 116th regular period of sessions, held from 7 to 25 October 2002), Articles 25, 31.

16 See Mental Disability Rights International, 'Human rights and mental health: Mexico' (Washington, DC, 2000); E. Rosenthal and E. Szeli, 'Not on the agenda: human rights of people with mental disabilities in Kosovo' (Washington, DC, 2002), both available via www.mdri.org/mdri-reports-publications.html (accessed 14 February 2009).

17 L. O. Gostin, 'Human rights in mental health: a proposal for five international standards based upon the Japanese experience', *International Journal of Law and Psychiatry* 10:4 (1987).

18 Cases, respectively, of *Winterwerp* v. *the Netherlands, B.* v. *the United Kingdom, Matter* v. *Slovakia*, and *Bock* v. *Germany*.

19 Cases of *Herczegfalvy* v. *Austria, J. T.* v. *the United Kingdom, Draper* v. *the United Kingdom*, and *K.* v. *Finland*.

20 *Additional Protocol to the American Convention on Human Rights in the Area of Economic, Social and Cultural Rights, 'Protocol Of San Salvador'*, San Salvador, 17 November 1988, OAS Treaty Series 69.

21 See L. O. Gostin, 'The right to health: a right to the "highest attainable standard of health"', *Hastings Center Report* 31 (March/April 2001).

22 P. Hunt, 'The UN Special Rapporteur on the right to health: key objectives, themes, and interventions', *Health and Human Rights* 7:1 (2003).

23 'The right of everyone to the enjoyment of the highest attainable standard of physical and mental health: report of the Special Rapporteur', United Nations Economic and Social Council Committee on Human Rights, 59th Session, Agenda Item 10, United Nations Document E/CN.4/2003/58 (2003).

24 'Report of the Special Rapporteur on the right of everyone to the enjoyment of the highest attainable standard of physical and mental health', United Nations Economic

and Social Council Committee on Human Rights, 61st Session, Agenda Item 10, United Nations Document E/CN.4/2005/51 (2005).

25 The World Health Organization (WHO) MIND Project; for information see www. who.int/mental_health/policy/en/ (accessed 14 February 2009).

26 M. Freeman and S. Pathare, *The WHO Resource Book on Mental Health, Human Rights and Legislation* (Geneva: World Health Organization, 2005).

27 G. Miller, 'The unseen: mental illness's global toll', *Science* 311 (2006).

28 A. Mastroeni, C. Bellotti, E. Pellegrini, F. Galletti, E. Lai and I. Falloon, 'Clinical and social outcomes five years after closing a mental hospital: a trial of cognitive behavioural interventions', *Clinical Practice and Epidemiology in Mental Health* 1:25 (2005).

29 P. White and H. Whiteford, 'Prisons: mental health institutions of the 21st century?' *Medical Journal of Australia* 185:6 (2006).

30 S. Fazel and J. Danesh, 'Serious mental disorder in 23,000 prisoners: a systematic review of 62 surveys', *Lancet* 359 (2002).

31 T. Butler, G. Andrews, S. Allnutt, C. Sakashita, N. E. Smith and J. Basson, 'Mental disorders in Australian prisoners: a comparison with a community sample', *Australian and New Zealand Journal of Psychiatry* 40:3 (2006).

32 S. Mohammad Assadi, M. Noroozian, M. Pakravannejad *et al.*, 'Psychiatric morbidity among sentenced prisoners: prevalence study in Iran', *British Journal of Psychiatry* 188 (2006).

33 P. M. Brinded, A. I. Simpson, T. M. Laidlaw, N. Fairley and F. Malcolm, 'Prevalence of psychiatric disorders in New Zealand prisons: a national study', *Australian and New Zealand Journal of Psychiatry* 35:2 (2001).

34 T. Brugha, N. Singleton, H. Meltzer *et al.*, 'Psychosis in the community and in prisons: a report from the British national survey of psychiatric morbidity', *American Journal of Psychiatry* 162:4 (2005).

35 D. J. James and L. E. Glaze, 'Mental health problems of prison and jail inmates' (Washington, DC: United States Department of Justice's Bureau of Justice Statistics, 2006).

36 L. M. Stewart, C. J. Henderson, M. S. Hobbs, S. C. Ridout and M. W. Knuiman, 'Risk of death in prisoners after release from jail', *Australian and New Zealand Journal of Public Health* 28:1 (2004).

3a Stephen Shute

Mental illness, preventive detention, prison, and human rights[1]

Throughout his long and distinguished career, Larry Gostin has campaigned tirelessly to improve the way modern societies treat those experiencing mental illness. In his essay for the Oxford Amnesty Lectures, Gostin again turns his attention to this topic. Using language that pulls no punches, he catalogues the appalling inhumanities that people with mental illness have had to endure and condemns what he describes as a 'vicious cycle of neglect, abandonment, indignity, cruel and inhumane treatment, and punishment'. On reaching the end of his account, few readers will be left without a strong sense of shame: for the maltreatment that the mentally ill have been subjected to over the years is something for which we all bear collective responsibility.

Mental illness, of course, varies in its impact and its intensity. In its most destructive form, it robs sufferers, either temporarily or permanently, of that which lies at the very core of their being: the general capacity to control their lives and to make them their own. But usually mental illness is less extreme and more confined than that, and often it is amenable to treatment. What all forms of mental illness have in common, however, is that they undermine, to a greater or lesser extent, the sufferer's ability to thrive in an increasingly complex and isolating world. Mental illness is also a condition that carries with it considerable societal stigma and is widely misunderstood, a point that was underscored in a 2009 United Kingdom poster campaign that featured the comic actor Stephen Fry. The campaign was built around the conceit that while Fry, like many other people, had a problem with mental illness, many more people seemed to have a problem with that.

At one time our communal response to the 'problem' of mental illness was to create what were in effect large holding pens for the mentally ill. Often dating back to Victorian times, these buildings were typically placed in remote rural locations: out of sight, out of mind. Unfortunately, their isolation only served to increase the likelihood of abuse. When these human 'warehouses' (to use Gostin's term) became so expensive and so dehumanising that they could no longer be tolerated, a new approach, so-called 'care in the community', was introduced. All too frequently, though, this new policy amounted to institutionalised neglect rather than delivering the compassion that had been promised. The community seemed not to want to know and the expected 'care' seldom materialised. The result, as Gostin powerfully explains, was that a strategy which had on its face espoused decarceration merely shifted a challenging population from one dehumanising institution, the asylum, to another, the prison.

Prisons, like asylums, are what Erving Goffman and Larry Gostin call 'total institutions'. They are places of confinement where all aspects of an inmate's life are controlled by the authorities. Like asylums, they have considerable potential for abuse. The larger and more overcrowded a prison gets, the greater the probability that this potential will be realised. Many Western democracies have had to confront this issue in recent times including the United Kingdom where the prison population has risen dramatically over the last two decades, driven by an uncomfortable combination of increased societal punitiveness and the belief that incarceration can keep citizens safe by stopping 'dangerous' people from committing serious crime.

However, our abilities to separate out accurately those persons who will commit serious criminal offences if allowed to remain in the community from those who will not are far less reliable than many suppose. Predicting human behaviour is never easy at the best of times but the task is made even more intractable when the behaviour one seeks to predict – serious violent or sexual reoffending – is that which is least likely to occur. An analogy can be drawn with the problem of predicting extreme weather conditions, such as hurricanes or tornados, or other exceptional natural events, such as tsunamis: nailing down in advance exactly when and where these events will occur is, given our current knowledge, a nigh on impossible task.

Take sexual reoffending as an example. The chances that a person convicted of a serious sexual offence will be reconvicted of a further sexual crime, even after a lengthy period in the community, are considerably lower than many people seem to think. Thus when Professor Roger Hood and I followed up a sample of serious sex offenders in England and Wales who had been released from sentences of long-term imprisonment, we found that less than 10 per cent were reconvicted for a further sexual crime even after six years in the community.[2] So while in the context of sexual offending the stakes are certainly high, the objective risks are relatively low. Our study also found that when Parole Board members assessed the danger posed by sex offenders, at least in the early 1990s, they judged many more of them to be 'high risk' than were in fact convicted of a further sexual crime during the six-year follow-up period. These Board members were particularly prone to over-estimate the risk of reconviction of sex offenders who had committed their crimes within their own family unit and the risk of reconviction of those who were 'denying' their offences.

Over time our ability to predict risks accurately may improve. But even if it develops to the point where it becomes infallible, arguments can be made against incarcerating people on the basis of what they will do in the future rather than on the basis of what they have done in the past. Many consider these arguments to be at their strongest when directed towards the preventive confinement of persons with mental illness. For, as Gostin rightly observes, the 'belief that persons with mental illness are uniformly dangerous is [a] . . . harmful myth'. Nonetheless, when all these arguments are considered, we may still conclude that some forms of preventive detention, even of the mentally ill, are justified as a way of limiting the risk posed to others by a small minority of people. If so, it is incumbent on us to ensure that those who are deprived of their liberty on the basis of their perceived danger are afforded at least the same level of protection for their human rights as other detainees, and arguably even greater protection.

In England and Wales, the rights of mentally ill prisoners fall under the same general regulatory regime that applies to all other prisoners. This is created by case law, legislation, the *European Convention on Human Rights and Freedoms*, and other international instruments that protect human rights. Legislation includes the Prison Act 1952 and the Prison Rules 1999 (and later amendments to these Rules) as well as various H.M. Prison Service Orders and Instructions which, taken together, establish a minimum set of standards for all held in prisons in England and Wales.[3] The rights they create cover a wide range of areas, including health, hygiene, food and nutrition, exercise, educational facilities, correspondence and visits, access to the media, and work.

So far as case law is concerned, the starting point is the decision taken more than a quarter of a century ago by the House of Lords in *Raymond* v. *Honey*[4] where it was held that 'a convicted prisoner, in spite of his imprisonment, retains all civil rights which are not taken away expressly or by necessary implication'. Similarly, the European Court of Human Rights has frequently observed that – with the exception of Article 5 of the Convention which expressly allows a state to curtail the right to liberty where a prisoner's detention has been authorised through a lawful legal process – there is 'no question' of a prisoner forfeiting his Convention rights 'merely because of his status as a person detained following conviction'.[5] Prisoners thus enjoy the same rights and freedoms under the Convention as other people and any restrictions imposed must be pursuant to a legitimate aim and be necessary in a democratic society to prevent crime, preserve prison security, protect the safety of prisoners or other individuals, or ensure good order and discipline. The broad position in English law, therefore, is that limitations may be placed on the rights of a prisoner but they must be necessary for one of the aforementioned purposes. Furthermore, where such limitations are imposed, they must be proportionate to the legitimate aims that the state is seeking to achieve.

Nonetheless, there are areas where the protection offered by the law to prisoners in England and Wales falls short of what might be regarded as a minimally acceptable position in other countries and what is required by international instruments. Let us begin by considering the right to health. In England and Wales the provision of healthcare in prisons is now the responsibility of the Department of Health which works in partnership with H.M. Prison Service. The goal is to provide prisoners with the same standard of care and treatment that is made available generally to British citizens under the National Health Service.[6] So far as mental health is concerned, the 'level of need' is, as the Deputy Director General of H.M. Prison Service has recently observed, 'typically high'. Indeed, 'surveys indicate that nine out of every ten prisoners have at least one of the following disorders: neurosis, psychosis, personality disorder, alcohol abuse or drug dependence'.[7] It is, therefore, disappointing that in her 2007–8 *Annual Report* H.M. Chief Inspector of Prisons for England and Wales stated that although mental health services for prisoners had improved, they were still 'often insufficient to meet the need'. So bad was the situation that she reported that in half of the male local and training prisons and all of the women's prisons she had inspected, primary mental healthcare was either 'non-existent or inadequate'.[8]

Regarding the right to physical welfare, it is a fundamental entitlement that all detained persons should have proper sleeping facilities. This is provided for in England and Wales by Rule 27 of the Prison Rules 1999, which states that every prisoner is required to 'be provided with a separate bed and with separate bedding adequate for warmth and health'.[9] Another fundamental requirement is adequate food. The relevant provision here is Rule 24 of the Prison Rules 1999 (as amended) which provides that the food provided to prisoners 'shall be wholesome, nutritious, well prepared and served, reasonably varied and sufficient in quantity'. In addition, paragraph 2.1 of Prison Service Order 5000 states that all prisoners 'must be provided with three meals per day – breakfast, lunch and evening or equivalent'; and paragraph 2.37 states that 'All religious, cultural and medical dietary needs must be met.'[10]

On the less positive side, the Prison Rules 1999 had the effect of downgrading the right that prisoners in England and Wales used to have under Rule 27 of the Prison Rules 1964 to a minimum of one hour's 'daily exercise' in the 'open air'.[11] Now they are entitled under Rule 30 only 'to be given the opportunity to spend time in the open air at least once every day, for such a period as may be reasonable in the circumstances'. This right is further circumscribed by a statement in the Rule that the entitlement is 'subject to the need to maintain good order and discipline'. On the other hand, prisoners are given a right under Rule 29 to have 'the opportunity to participate in physical education for at least one hour per week' although this right too is qualified by the expression 'if circumstances reasonably permit'.

The right of prisoners in England and Wales to education is governed by Rules 32 and 33 of the Prison Rules 1999. These establish a general duty on the part of prisons to provide education but do not create the right for prisoners to demand any specific educational provision. Instead, they leave a broad discretion in the hands of the authorities as to what form prison education should take. Rule 32, for example, states that 'reasonable facilities shall be afforded to prisoners who wish to do so to improve their education by training by distance learning, private study and recreational classes, in their spare time'; and Rule 33 states that 'every prisoner shall be allowed to have library books and to exchange them'. In each case, these rights are qualified by the expression 'subject to any directions of the Secretary of State'.

The entitlement of prisoners in England and Wales to have visits and to send and receive correspondence receives some protection from Article 8 (right to private and family life) and Article 10 (right to freedom of expression) of the *European Convention on Human Rights and Freedoms*. Correspondence to and from persons held in prisons in England and Wales is also protected by Prison Service Order 4411, which establishes that censorship of a prisoner's mail should occur only where it is deemed strictly necessary while allowing for the routine reading of the mail for all prisoners who pose the highest security risk.[12] But there is no right for prisoners in England and Wales to have access to email. Nor is there an absolute right of access to a telephone, although in practice every prison in England and Wales has telephone facilities that can be used by prisoners. With the exception of calls to legal advisers and certain other designated organisations, all calls by and to prisoners may be monitored and recorded by the prison authorities.

Regarding work, the Prison Rules do not provide prisoners held in custodial establishments in England and Wales with a right to guaranteed work but where work is done by prisoners they have the right to be paid at rates set by the prison governor, subject to the minimum level established by Prison Service Order 4460 of £4.00 for a five-day week.[13] Under Prison Rule 31, convicted prisoners may be required to do useful work for not more than ten hours a day.

Finally, it is worth saying something about the unsatisfactory position of prisoners in the UK in relation to the right to vote. Sentenced prisoners were disenfranchised by the Forfeiture Act 1870 on the ground that those serving a custodial sentence should be regarded as 'civically dead'. This view was later affirmed by the Representation of the People Act 1969, the Representation of the People Act 1983, and the Representation of the People Act 2000.[14] However, in 2005 the European Court of Human Rights held in *Hirst* v. *the United Kingdom* that the UK's legislative provisions on prisoner voting were incompatible with Article 3 of the First Protocol to the European Convention.[15] Although the Court left open the possibility that certain classes of prisoner, such as those who had seriously abused a public or official position or those whose conduct had threatened to undermine the rule of law or a state's democratic foundations, might lawfully be disenfranchised, the blanket ban that operated in the UK on convicted prisoners voting was regarded as an 'automatic and indiscriminate restriction on a vitally important Convention right' and 'outside any acceptable margin of appreciation' that the UK might have in implementing the Convention.

A sea change in attitude was therefore required in order to bring the UK's legislation on prisoner voting into line with the country's obligations under the European Convention. Yet the UK Government has shown little enthusiasm for implementing the *Hirst* ruling. Its only formal response to date has been to issue a Consultation Paper on the 'Voting rights of convicted prisoners detained within the United Kingdom'.[16] This document, which was published on 14 December 2006, restated the Government's 'firm belief' that 'individuals who have committed an offence serious enough to warrant a term of imprisonment should not be able to vote while in prison'. It also noted that the *Hirst* judgment did not mean 'that the Government must enfranchise all prisoners'. The Government's unwillingness to implement *Hirst* was further reflected in the options for change that were set out in the document. These did not offer total enfranchisement as an option but did invite comments on total disenfranchisement despite acknowledging that this option was incompatible with the ruling in *Hirst*.

The consultation established by the December 2006 paper closed in March 2007. It was envisaged as the first part of a two-stage consultative process. But, in response to a parliamentary question from Lord Pannick in the House of Lords in December 2008, the Parliamentary Under-Secretary of State in the Ministry of Justice, Lord Bach, told peers that he could not tell them when the second stage of the consultation might begin. He also reminded peers of the foreword to the December 2006 paper, written by Lord Falconer, the then Lord Chancellor, which said that 'Successive UK Governments have held to the view that the right to vote forms part of the social contract between individuals and the State, and that loss of the right to vote, reflected in the current law, is a proper and proportionate punishment for breaches of the social contract that resulted in imprisonment.'[17]

It is clear, then, that we should not expect any change to the current UK law on prisoners' voting rights in the near future, even though the UK's approach is out of line with its obligations under international law. All of which merely serves to underscore Gostin's observation that 'international human rights norms will have maximum impact only if they are adopted by nations into domestic laws, policies and programmes'.

Notes

1 The author would like to thank Paul Mora for helping check some of the references and Julia Shute for her helpful comments on a first draft of the essay. Editor's note: this essay was written in February 2009.

2 See Roger Hood, Stephen Shute, Martina Feilzer and Aidan Wilcox, 'Sex offenders emerging from long-term imprisonment', *British Journal of Criminology* 42:2 (2002).

3 UK Acts and Statutory Instruments, such as the Prison Rules, can be found via www.opsi.gov.uk/legislation/uk. Prison Service Orders and Prison Service Instructions can be found via www.hmprisonservice.gov.uk/resourcecentre/psispsos/ (both accessed 30 June 2009).

4 [1983] 1 AC 1, *per* Lord Wilberforce.

5 See *Hirst* v. *the United Kingdom* (Application No. 74025/01) (2006) 42 EHRR 41 cited in *Dickson* v. *the United Kingdom* (Application No. 44362/04) (2007) 44 EHRR 21.

6 See the Prison Service Standard on Health Services for Prisoners (May 2004), which is to 'provide prisoners with access to the same range and quality of services as the general public receives from the NHS', available via www.dh.gov.uk/en/Publicationsandstatistics/Publications/PublicationsPolicyAndGuidance/DH_077037 (accessed 30 June 2009).

7 Michael Spurr, 'Background on the English and Welsh prison system', in Peter Tak and Manon Jendly (eds), *Prison Policy and Prisoners' Rights* (Nijmegen: Wolf Legal Publishers, 2008).

8 *H.M. Chief Inspector of Prisons for England and Wales, Annual Report 2007–08*, HC 118, January 2009, p. 29.

9 Statutory Instrument 1999 No. 728, The Prison Rules 1999 (The Stationery Office).

10 PSO 5000, issue no. 294, issued 9 April 2008.

11 Statutory Instrument 1964 No. 388, The Prison Rules 1964 (The Stationery Office).

12 PSO 4411, issue no. 280, issued 5 September 2007.

13 See Annex B to PSO 4460, issue no. 142, 7 January 2000.

14 The Representation of the People Act 2000 gave remand prisoners and unconvicted mental patients the right to vote.

15 (Application No. 74025/01) (2006) 42 EHRR 41.

16 *The UK Government's response to the Grand Chamber of the European Court of Human Rights judgment in the case of Hirst v The United Kingdom*. Consultation Paper CP29/06. The consultation began on 14 December 2006 and ended on 7 March 2007.

17 House of Lords Debates, 15 December 2008.

Part II:

Beyond the prison

The use and abuse of the prison in the age of social insecurity

In this essay, I draw selectively on my three books on the nexus of penality, poverty and politics to present the skeleton of an argument explaining the expansion and glorification of the penal mission of the state in the early twenty-first century as *part and parcel of the neoliberal revolution* and *an exercise in state-crafting*.[1] The prison boom we are witnessing around the world today, qualifying as the 'third age' of carceral expansion after the historic bursts of the early seventeenth century and the mid-nineteenth century, is not a response to trends in crime, but a core component of the remaking of Leviathan designed to contain the social and mental insecurity that the state itself has fostered by deregulating the economy and dismantling the social safety net woven under the Fordist-Keynesian compact. So much to say, in response to the programme notes of the Oxford Amnesty Lectures 2007 series, that I do not see the prison as a 'barometer for the theory and implementation of human rights', for social history and comparative anthropology teach us that the prison is itself an *outlaw institution*: an instrument of coercion that concentrates deviance and violence in a separate physical space which invisibilises the problem categories, conditions and conducts that the society does not wish to confront by other means.[2] On a day-to-day level, the carceral institution necessarily and routinely violates the very laws it is presumed to uphold to rule over populations recalcitrant to the social and moral order. Fyodor Dostoyevsky is famously quoted as saying that the state of prisons reveals the 'degree of *civilization* in a society' (emphasis added). I argue instead that it indicates the *kind of state* that a society has built and the degree of state lawlessness it tolerates in the political management of inequality and marginality. This is for a very simple reason: everywhere the prison is a people-processing organisation virtually reserved for the vulnerable segments of the lower class, the dispossessed and the dishonoured.

To arrive at a proper diagnosis of the expansive use and abuse of the prison in the age of economic deregulation and social insecurity, it is imperative that we effect three analytic breaks with the gamut of established approaches to incarceration. First, we must decouple crime from punishment, in light of the glaring and persistent disconnect between trends and levels in offences and sanctions both within and across countries. Second, we must recouple social and penal policies, insofar as these two strands of public action were historically fashioned in tandem and are everywhere aimed at the same populations residing in the nether regions of social and physical space. And, third, we must move from a repressive to a productive conception of penal power that enables us to construe the prison as a core political capacity that is generative of social reality through the fusion of material and symbolic modalities of action. Premised on these three principles, the comparative analysis of penal trends and discourses in the advanced countries over the past decade reveals a close link between the ascendancy of neoliberalism, as ideological project and governmental practice mandating submission to the 'free market' and the celebration of 'individual responsibility' in all realms, on the one hand, and the deployment of punitive and proactive law-enforcement policies targeting street delinquency and the categories trapped in the margins and cracks of the new economic and moral order, on the other hand. Beyond their national inflections and institutional variations, these policies sport six common features.[3]

First, they purport to put an end to the 'era of leniency' and to attack head-on the problem of crime, as well as urban disorders and the public nuisances bordering the confines of penal law, baptised 'incivilities', while deliberately disregarding their causes. Whence, second, a proliferation of laws and an insatiable craving for bureaucratic innovations and technological gadgets: crime-watch groups and partnerships between the police and other public services (schools, hospitals, social workers, the national tax office, etc.); video surveillance cameras and computerised mapping of offences; compulsory drug testing, 'tazer' and 'flash-ball' guns; fast-track judicial processing and the extension of the prerogatives of probation and parole officers; criminal profiling, satellite-aided electronic monitoring, and generalised genetic fingerprinting; enlargement and technological modernisation of carceral facilities; multiplication of specialised custodial centres (for foreigners awaiting expulsion, recidivist minors, women and the sick, convicts serving community sentences, etc.). Third, the need for this punitive turn is everywhere conveyed by an alarmist, even catastrophist discourse on 'insecurity' animated with martial images and broadcast to saturation by the commercial media, the major political parties, and professionals in the enforcement of order – police officials, magistrates, legal scholars, experts and merchants in 'urban safety' services – who vie to propose remedies as drastic as they are simplistic. Fourth, out of a proclaimed concern for efficiency in the 'war on crime' and solicitude towards this new figure of the deserving citizen that is the crime victim, this discourse openly revalorises repression and stigmatises youths from declining working-class neighbourhoods, the jobless, homeless, beggars, drug addicts and street prostitutes, and immigrants from the former colonies of the West and from the ruins of the Soviet empire. Fifth, on the carceral front, the therapeutic philosophy of 'rehabilitation' has been more or less supplanted by a managerialist approach centred on the cost-driven administration of carceral stocks and flows, paving the way for the privatisation of correctional services. Lastly, the implementation of these new punitive policies has invariably resulted in an extension and tightening of the police dragnet, a hardening and speeding-up of judicial procedures, and, at the end of the penal chain, an incongruous increase in the population under lock, without anyone seriously addressing the question of these policies' financial burden, social costs and civic implications.

These punitive policies are the object of an unprecedented political consensus and enjoy broad public support cutting across class lines boosted by the blurring of crime, poverty and immigration in the media, as well as by the constant confusion between insecurity and the 'feeling of insecurity'. This confusion is tailor-made to channel towards the (dark-skinned) figure of the street delinquent the diffuse anxiety caused by a string of interrelated social changes: the dislocations of wage work, the crisis of the patriarchal family and the erosion of traditional relations of authority among sex and age categories, the decomposition of established working-class territories, and the intensification of school competition as require- ment for access to employment. Penal severity is now presented virtually everywhere and by everyone as a healthy necessity, a vital reflex of self-defence by a social body threatened by the gangrene of criminality, no matter how petty. The grand American experiment of the 'war on crime' has also imposed itself as the manda- tory reference for the governments of the First World, the theoretical source and practical inspiration for the general hardening of penality that has translated in all advanced countries into a spectacular swelling of the population behind bars.[4] Caught in the vice of the biased alternative between catastrophic and angelic visions, anyone who dares to question the self-evident commonplaces of the *pensée unique* about 'insecurity' that now rules uncontested is irrevocably (dis)qualified as a vain dreamer or an ideologue guilty of ignoring the harsh realities of contemporary urban life.

The generalisation of social insecurity and its effects

The sudden growth and glorification of the penal state in the United States, starting in the mid-1970s, and then in Western Europe two decades later, does not correspond to a rupture in the evolution of crime and delinquency – the scale and physiognomy of offending did not change abruptly at the start of the two periods in question on either side of the Atlantic. Neither does it translate a leap in the efficiency of the repressive apparatus that would justify its reinforcement, as zealots of the scholarly myth of 'zero tolerance' now spread around the world would have us believe. It is not criminality that has changed here so much as the *gaze that society trains on certain street illegalities*, that is, in the final analysis, *on the dispossessed*

and dishonoured populations (by status or origin) that are their presumed perpetra-
tors, on the place that they occupy in the City, and on the uses to which these
populations can be subjected in the political and journalistic fields.

These castaway categories – unemployed youth and the homeless, aimless
nomads and drug addicts, postcolonial immigrants without documents or support
– have become salient in public space, their presence undesirable and their doings
intolerable, because they are the living and threatening incarnation of the generalised
social insecurity produced both by the erosion of stable and homogeneous wage
work (promoted to the rank of paradigm of employment during the decades of
Fordist expansion in 1945–1975), and by the decomposition of the solidarities
of class and culture that this stable employment underpinned within a clearly
circumscribed national framework.[5] Just as national boundaries have been blurred
by the hypermobility of capital, the settlement of migration flows and European
integration, the normalisation of desocialised labour feeds a powerful current of
anxiety in all the societies of the continent. This current mixes the fear of the future,
the dread of social decline and degradation, and the anguish of not being able to
transmit one's status to one's offspring in a competition for credentials and
positions that is ever more intense and uncertain. It is this diffuse and multifaceted
social and mental insecurity, which (objectively) strikes working-class families
shorn of the cultural capital required to accede to the protected sectors of the labour
market, and (subjectively) haunts large sectors of the middle class, that the new
martial discourse of politicians and the media on delinquency has captured, fixating
it on to the narrow issue of physical or criminal insecurity.

To understand how the law-and-order upsurge that has swept through postin-
dustrial countries around the close of the century constitutes a *reaction to, a diversion
from and a denegation of, the generalisation of the social and mental insecurity*
produced by the diffusion of desocialised wage labour against the backdrop of
increased inequality, one must break with the ritual opposition of intellectual
schools and wed the virtues of a *materialist* analysis, inspired by Marx and Engels,
and the strengths of a *symbolic* approach, initiated by Emile Durkheim and
amplified by Pierre Bourdieu. The materialist perspective, elaborated by various
strands of radical criminology, is attuned to the changing relations that obtain in
each epoch (and particularly during phases of socioeconomic upheaval) between
the penal system and the system of production, while the symbolic outlook is
attentive to the capacity that the state has to trace salient social demarcations
and produce social reality through its work of inculcation of efficient categories and
classifications.[6] The traditionally hostile separation of these two approaches, the one
stressing the instrumental role of penality as a vector of power and the other its
expressive mission and integrative capacity, is but an accident of academic history
artificially sustained by stale intellectual politics. It is imperative that this separation be overcome, for in historical reality penal institutions and policies can and

do shoulder both tasks at once: they simultaneously act to enforce hierarchy and control contentious categories, at one level, and to communicate norms and shape collective representations and subjectivities, at another.[7] The police, courts and prison are not mere technical implements whereby the authorities respond to crime – as in the commonsensical view fostered by law and criminology – but a core political capacity through which the state both produces and manages inequality, identity and marginality.

Indeed, the generalised hardening of police, judicial and correctional policies that can be observed in most of the countries of the First World over the past two decades[8] partakes of a *triple transformation of the state*, which it helps simultaneously to accelerate and obfuscate, wedding the amputation of its economic arm, the retraction of its social bosom, and the massive expansion of its penal fist. This transformation is the bureaucratic response of political elites to the mutations of wage work (a shift to services and polarisation of jobs, the flexibilisation and intensification of work, the individualisation of employment contracts, the discontinuity and dispersion of occupational paths) and their ravaging effects on the lower tiers of the social and spatial structure. These mutations themselves are the product of a swing in the balance of power between the classes and groups that struggle at every moment for control over the worlds of employment. And in this struggle, it is the transnational business class and the 'modernising' fractions of the cultural bourgeoisie and high state nobility, allied under the banner of neoliberalism, that have gained the upper hand and embarked on a sweeping campaign to reconstruct public power in line with their material and symbolic interests.[9]

The commodification of public goods and the rise of underpaid, insecure work against the backdrop of working poverty in the United States and enduring mass joblessness in the European Union; the unravelling of social protection schemes, leading to the replacement of the collective right to recourse against unemployment and destitution by the individual obligation to take up gainful activity ('workfare' in the US and the UK, ALE jobs in Belgium, PARE and RMA in France, the Hartz reform in Germany, etc.), in order to impose desocialised wage labour as the normal horizon of work for the new proletariat of the urban service sectors;[10] and the reinforcement and extension of the punitive apparatus, recentred on to the dispossessed districts of the inner city and the urban periphery, into which are concentrated the disorders and despair spawned by the twofold movement of retrenchment of the state from the economic and social front: these three trends implicate and intricate one another in a self-perpetuating causal chain that is redrawing the perimeter and redefining the modalities of government action.

The Keynesian state, coupled with Fordist wage work operating as a spring of *solidarity*, whose mission was to counter the recessive cycles of the market economy, protect the most vulnerable populations, and curb glaring inequalities, has been succeeded by a state that one might dub *neo-Darwinist*, in that it erects

competition to the rank of fetish and celebrates unrestrained individual responsibility
– whose counterpart is collective and thus political irresponsibility. The Leviathan
withdraws into its regalian functions of law enforcement, themselves hypertrophied
and deliberately abstracted from their social environment, and into its symbolic
mission to reassert common values through the public anathematisation of deviant
categories, chief among them the unemployed 'street thug' and the 'paedophile',
viewed as the walking incarnations of the abject failure to live up to the abstemious
ethic of wage work and sexual self-control. Unlike its *belle époque* predecessor, this
new-style Darwinism, which praises the 'winners' for their vigour and intelligence,
and vituperates the 'losers' in the 'struggle for economic life' by pointing to their
character flaws and behavioural deficiencies, does not find its model in nature.[11]
It is the market that supplies it with its master-metaphor and the mechanism of
selection supposed to ensure the 'survival of the fittest' – but only after the market
itself has been naturalised, that is to say, depicted under radically dehistoricised
trappings which, paradoxically, turn it into a concrete historical realisation of the
pure and perfect abstractions of the orthodox economic science which is promoted
to the rank of official theodicy of the social order *in statu nascendi*.

   Thus the 'invisible hand' of the unskilled labour market, strengthened by the
shift from welfare to workfare, finds its ideological extension and institutional
complement in the 'iron fist' of the penal state, which grows and redeploys in order
to *stem the disorders generated by the diffusion of social insecurity* and by the correlative
destabilisation of the status hierarchies that formed the traditional framework of
the national society (i.e., the division between whites and blacks in the United States
and between nationals and colonial immigrants in Western Europe). The regulation of the working classes through what Pierre Bourdieu calls 'the Left hand' of
the state,[12] that which protects and expands life chances, represented by labour law,
education, health, social assistance, and public housing, is *supplanted* (in the US)
or *supplemented* (in the EU) by regulation through its 'Right hand', that of the police,
justice, and correctional administrations, increasingly active and intrusive in the
subaltern zones of social and urban space. And, logically, the prison returns to the
forefront of the societal stage, when only thirty years ago the most eminent
specialists of the penal question were unanimous in predicting its waning, if not its
disappearance.[13]

   The renewed utility of the penal apparatus in the post-Keynesian era of
insecure employment is threefold: (i) it works to bend the fractions of the working
class recalcitrant to the discipline of the new, fragmented, service wage labour by
increasing the cost of strategies of exit into the informal economy of the street;
(ii) it neutralises and warehouses its most disruptive elements, or those rendered
wholly superfluous by the recomposition of the demand for labour; and (iii) it
reaffirms the authority of the state in daily life within the restricted domain hence-
forth assigned to it. The canonisation of the 'right to security', correlative to the

dereliction of the 'right to employment' in its old form (that is, full-time and with full benefits, for an indefinite period and for a living wage enabling one to reproduce oneself socially and to project oneself into the future), and the increased interest in and resources granted to the enforcement of order come at just the right time to shore up the deficit of legitimacy suffered by political decision-makers, owing to the very fact that they have abjured the established missions of the state on the social and economic fronts.

Under these conditions, one understands better why, throughout Europe, the parties of the governmental Left smitten with the neoliberal vision have proven so fond of the security thematics incarnated by 'zero tolerance' imported from the United States in the past decade, or its British cousins such as 'community policing'. For, in their case, the adoption of policies of economic deregulation and social retrenchment amounts to a political betrayal of the working-class electorate that brought them to power in the hope of receiving stronger state protection against the sanctions and failings of the market. Thus the punitive turn taken by Lionel Jospin in France in the fall of 1997, like those negotiated by Anthony Blair in Britain, Felipe González in Spain, Massimo d'Alema in Italy, and Gerhard Schröder in Germany around the same years, after William Jefferson Clinton had plainly adopted the ultra-punitive agenda of the Republican Party in the US in 1994,[14] has little to do with the alleged 'explosion' in youth delinquency or with the 'urban violence' that has invaded public debate towards the end of the past decade. It has everything to do with the generalisation of desocialised wage labour and the establishment of a political regime that will facilitate its imposition. It is a regime that one may call 'liberal-paternalist', insofar as it is *liberal* and permissive at the top, with regard to corporations and the upper class, and *paternalist* and authoritarian at the bottom, towards those who find themselves caught between the restructuring of employment, and the ebbing of social protection or its conversion into an instrument of surveillance and discipline.

When prisonfare joins welfare: the double regulation of the poor

The resolutely punitive turn taken by penal policies in advanced societies at the close of the twentieth century thus does not pertain to the simple diptych of 'crime and punishment'. It heralds the establishment of a *new government of social insecurity*, 'in the expansive sense of techniques and procedures aimed at directing the conduct of the men' and women caught up in the turbulence of economic deregulation and the conversion of welfare into a springboard towards precarious employment,[15] an organisational design within which the prison assumes a major role and which translates, for the categories residing in the nether regions of social space, into the imposition of severe and supercilious supervision. It is the United States that invented this new politics of poverty during the period from 1973 to 1996, in the wake of the social, racial and anti-statist reaction to the progressive movements of the preceding decade that was to be the crucible of the neoliberal revolution.[16]

The explosive rise of the carceral sector in the United States, where the confined population has quadrupled in two decades to exceed 2.2 million, even as the crime rate stagnated and then declined, partakes of a broader restructuring of the US bureaucratic field tending to criminalise poverty and its consequences so as to anchor precarious wage work as a new norm of citizenship at the bottom of the class structure, while remedying the derailing of the traditional mechanisms for maintaining the ethno-racial order. The planned atrophy of the social state, culminating with the 1996 law on 'Work Opportunity and Personal Responsibility', which replaced the right to 'welfare' with the obligation of 'workfare', and the sudden hypertrophy of the penal state are two concurrent and complementary developments. Each in its manner, they respond, on the one side, to the forsaking of the Fordist wage work compact and the Keynesian compromise in the mid-1970s, and, on the other side, to the crisis of the ghetto as a device for the sociospatial confinement of blacks in the wake of the Civil Rights Revolution and the wave of urban riots of the 1960s. Together, they ensnare the marginal populations of the metropolis in a *carceral-assistantial net* that aims either to render them 'useful' by steering them on to the track of deskilled employment through moral retraining and material suasion, or to warehouse them out of reach in the devastated core of the urban 'Black Belt' or in the penitentiaries that have become the latter's distant yet direct satellites.[17]

Social scientists and activists, as well as the politicians, professionals and activists who wish for reform, continue to approach social policy and penal policy as separate and isolated domains of public action, whereas in reality they already function in tandem at the bottom of the structure of classes and places. Just as the close of the nineteenth century witnessed the gradual disjunction of the social question from the penal question under the press of working-class mobilisation and the reconfiguration of the state it stimulated, the close of the twentieth century has been the theatre of a renewed fusion and confusion of these two issues, following the fragmentation of the world of the working class – its industrial dismantlement and the deepening of its internal divisions, its defensive retreat into the private sphere and crushing feeling of downward drift, its loss of a sense of collective dignity, and, lastly, its abandonment by Left parties more concerned with the games internal to their apparatus leading to its near disappearance from the public scene as a collective actor. It follows that the fight against street delinquency now serves as screen and counterpart to the new social question, namely, the generalisation of insecure wage work and its impact on the territories and life strategies of the urban proletariat.

In 1971, Frances Fox Piven and Richard Cloward published their classic book, *Regulating the Poor*, in which they argue that 'relief programs are initiated to deal with dislocations in the work system that lead to mass disorder, and are then retained (in an altered form) to enforce work'.[18] Thirty years later, this cyclical dynamic of expansion and contraction of public aid has been superseded by a new division of the labour of nomination and domination of deviant and dependent populations that couples welfare services and criminal justice administration under the aegis of the same behaviourist and punitive philosophy. The activation of disciplinary programmes applied to the unemployed, the indigent, single mothers, and others 'on assistance' so as to push them on to the peripheral sectors of the employment market, on the one side, and the deployment of an extended police and penal net with a reinforced mesh in the dispossessed districts of the metropolis, on the other side, are the two components of a single apparatus for the management of poverty that aims at effecting the authoritarian rectification of the behaviours of populations recalcitrant to the emerging economic and symbolic order. Failing which it aims to ensure the civic or physical expurgation of those who prove to be 'incorrigible' or useless. And, much as the development of modern 'welfare' in the United States, from its origins in the New Deal to the contemporary period, was decisively shaped by its entailment in a rigid and pervasive structure of racial domination that precluded the deployment of inclusive and universalist programmes, so too was the expansion of the penal state after the mid-1970s both dramatically accelerated and decisively twisted by the revolt and involutive collapse of the dark ghetto as well as by the subsequent ebbing of public support for black demands for civic equality.[19]

In the era of fragmented and discontinuous wage work, the regulation of working-class households is no longer handled solely by the maternal and nurturing social arm of the welfare state; it relies also on the virile and controlling arm of the penal state. The 'dramaturgy of labour' is not played solely on the stages of the public aid office and job-placement bureau, as Piven and Cloward insist in the 1993 revision of their classic. At century's turn, it also unfolds its stern scenarios in police stations, in the corridors of criminal courts, and in the darkness of prison cells.[20] This dynamic coupling of the Left and Right hands of the state operates through a familiar sharing of the roles between the sexes. The public aid bureaucracy, now reconverted into an administrative springboard into poverty-level employment, takes up the mission of inculcating the duty of working for work's sake among poor women (and indirectly their children): 90 per cent of welfare recipients in the US are mothers. The quartet formed by the police, the court, the prison, and the probation or parole officer assumes the task of taming their brothers, their boyfriends or husbands, and their sons: 93 per cent of US inmates are male (men also make up 88 per cent of parolees and 77 per cent of probationers). This suggests, in line with a rich strand of feminist scholarship on public policy, gender and citizenship,[21] that the invention of the *double regulation of the poor* in America in the closing decades of the twentieth century partakes of an overall (re)*masculinising of the state* in the neoliberal age, which is in part an oblique reaction to (or against) the social changes wrought by the women's movement and their reverberations inside the bureaucratic field.

Within this sexual and institutional division in the regulation of the poor, the 'clients' of both the assistantial and penitential sectors of the state fall under the same principled suspicion: they are considered morally deficient unless they periodically provide visible proof to the contrary. This is why their behaviours must be supervised and rectified by the imposition of rigid protocols whose violation will expose them to a redoubling of corrective discipline and, if necessary, to sanctions that can result in durable segregation, a manner of social death for moral failing – casting them outside the civic community of those entitled to social rights in the case of public aid recipients, outside the society of 'free' men for convicts. Welfare provision and criminal justice are now animated by the same punitive and paternalist philosophy that stresses the 'individual responsibility' of the 'client', treated in the manner of a 'subject', in contraposition to the universal rights and obligations of the citizen,[22] and they reach publics of roughly comparable size. In 2001, the number of households receiving Temporary Assistance to Needy Families, the main assistance programme established by the 1996 'welfare reform', was 2.1 million, corresponding to some 6 million beneficiaries. That the same year, the carceral population reached 2.1 million, but the total number of 'beneficiaries' of criminal justice supervision (tallying up inmates, probationers and parolees) was in the neighbourhood of 6.5 million. Moreover, welfare recipients and inmates have germane social profiles and extensive mutual ties that make them the two gendered sides of the same population coin.

A 'European road' to the penal state

Excavating the economic underpinnings and the socioracial dynamics of the rise of the penal state in the United States offers indispensable materials for a historical anthropology of the invention of neoliberalism in action. Since the rupture of the mid-1970s, this country has been the theoretical and practical motor for the elaboration and global dissemination of a political project that aims to subordinate all human activities to the tutelage of the market. Far from being an incidental or teratological development, the hypertrophic expansion of the penal sector of the bureaucratic field is an essential element of this field's new anatomy in the age of economic neo-Darwinism. To journey across the US carceral archipelago, then, is not only to travel to the 'extreme limits of European civilization', to borrow the words of Alexis de Tocqueville. It is also to discover the likely contours of the future landscape of the police, justice and prison in the European and Latin American countries that have embarked on the path of 'liberating' the economy and reconstructing the state blazed by the American leader. In this perspective, the United

States appears as a sort of historical alembic in which one can observe on a real scale, and anticipate by way of *structural transposition*, the social, political and cultural consequences of the advent of neoliberal penality in a society submitted to the joint empire of the commodity form and moralising individualism.

For the United States has not been content to be the forge and locomotive of the neoliberal project on the level of the economy and welfare; over the past decade, it has also become the premier global exporter of 'theories', slogans and measures on the crime and safety front.[23] In her panorama of carceral evolution around the planet, Vivien Stern stresses that 'a major influence on penal policy in Britain and other Western European countries has been the policy direction taken in the United States', an influence to which she attributes 'the complete reversal of the consensus prevailing in the postwar developed world and expressed in UN documents and international conventions' that 'deprivation of liberty should be used sparingly', and the general discrediting of the ideal of 'the rehabilitation and social reintegration of the offender'.[24] Whether through importation or inspiration, the alignment of penal policies never entails the deployment of identical replicas. In European countries with a strong statist tradition, Catholic or social-democratic, the new politics of poverty does not imply a mechanical duplication of the US pattern, with a clear and brutal swing from the social to the penal treatment of urban marginality leading to hyperincarceration. The deep roots of the social state in the bureaucratic fields and national mental structures, the weaker hold of the individualist and utilitarian ideology that undergirds the sacralisation of the market, and the absence of a sharp ethnoracial divide explain the fact that the countries of the European continent are unlikely to shift rapidly to an all-out punitive strategy. Each must clear its own path towards the new government of social insecurity in accordance with its specific national history, social configurations and political traditions. Nonetheless, one can sketch a provisional characterisation of a 'European road' to the penal state (with French, Dutch, Italian, etc., variants) that is gradually coming into being before our eyes through a *double and conjoint accentuation of the social and penal regulation of marginal categories*.

Thus, during the past decade, the French authorities have stepped up both welfare and justice interventions. On the one side, they have multiplied assistance programmes (public utility jobs, subsidised youth employment, training schemes, etc.), raised the various 'social minima' (targeted government aid to various destitute categories), established universal medical coverage, and broadened access to the Revenu Minimum d'Insertion (RMI, the guaranteed minimum income grant). On the other, they have created special surveillance units ('*cellules de veille*') and nested emergency riot police squads inside the 'sensitive zones' of the urban periphery; replaced street educators with magistrates to issue warnings to occasional youth delinquents; passed municipal decrees outlawing begging and vagrancy (even though such proscription is patently illegal); multiplied 'crackdown' operations and sweeps inside low-income housing projects, and made routine the use of *'comparution immédiate'* (a fast-track judicial procedure whereby an offender caught in the act is deferred before a judge and sentenced within hours); increased penalties for repeated offences; restricted parole release and speeded up the deportation of convicted foreign offenders; threatened the parents of juvenile delinquents or children guilty of school truancy with withholding family benefits, etc.

A second contrast between the United States and the countries of continental Europe is that penalisation *à l'européenne* is effected mainly through *the agency of the police and the courts rather than the prison*. It still obeys a predominantly panoptic logic, rather than a segregative and retributive rationale. The correlate is that social services play an active part in this criminalising process, since they possess the administrative and human means to exercise a close-up supervision of so-called problem populations. But the simultaneous deployment of the social and penal treatment of urban disorders should not hide the fact that the former often functions as a bureaucratic fig leaf for the latter, and that it is ever more directly subordinated to it in practice. Encouraging state social assistance, health and education services to collaborate with the police and judicial system turns them into extensions of the penal apparatus, instituting a *social panopticism* which, under cover of promoting the well-being of deprived populations, submits them to an ever more precise and penetrating form of punitive surveillance.

It remains to be seen whether this 'European road' to liberal paternalism is a genuine alternative to penalisation in the mould of the United States or merely an intermediate stage or detour leading, in the end, to carceral hyperinflation. If neighbourhoods of relegation are saturated with police without enhancing employment opportunities and life chances in them, and if partnerships between the criminal justice system and other state services are multiplied, there is bound to be an increase in the detection of unlawful conduct and an increased volume of arrests and convictions in criminal court. Who can say today where and when the ballooning of the jails and penitentiaries visible in nearly all the European countries will stop? The case of the Netherlands, which has shifted from a humanist to a managerial penal philosophy and gone from laggard to leader in incarceration among the original fifteen members of the European Union, is instructive and worrisome in this regard.[25]

The penalisation of poverty as production of reality

Just as the emergence of a new government of the social insecurity diffused by the neoliberal revolution does not mark a historical reversion to a familiar organisational configuration, but heralds a genuine political innovation, so too the deployment of the penal state cannot be grasped under the narrow rubric of repression. In point of fact, the repressive trope is a central ingredient in the discursive fog that enshrouds and masks the sweeping makeover of the means, ends and justifications of public authority at century's close. The leftist activists who rail against the 'punishment machine' on both sides of the Atlantic – castigating the chimerical 'prison-industrial complex' in America and denouncing a diabolical *'programme sécuritaire'* in France – mistake the wrapping for the package.[26] They fail to see that crime-fighting is but a convenient pretext and propitious platform for a broader redrawing of the perimeter of responsibility of the state, operating simultaneously on the economic, social welfare and penal fronts.

To realise that the rise of the punitive apparatus in advanced society pertains less to crime-fighting than to *state-crafting*, one must reject the conspiratorial view of history that would attribute it to a deliberate plan pursued by omniscient and omnipotent rulers, whether they be political decision-makers, corporate heads or the gamut of profiteers who benefit from the increased scope and intensity of punishment and related supervisory programmes trained on the urban cast-offs of deregulation. With Pierre Bourdieu, one must recuse the 'functionalism of the worst case' which casts all historical developments as the work of an omniscient strategist or as automatically beneficial to some abstract machinery of domination and exploitation that would 'reproduce' itself no matter what.[27] Such a vision not only confuses the objective convergence of a welter of disparate public policies, each driven by its own set of protagonists and stakes, with the subjective intentions of state managers. It also fails to heed Foucault's advice that we forsake the 'repressive hypothesis' and treat power as a fertilising force that remakes the very landscape it traverses.[28] Interestingly, this is an insight that one finds in Karl Marx's erstwhile dispersed remarks on crime, which suggest that the advent of 'liberal paternalism' is best construed under the generative category of *production*:

> The criminal produces an impression now moral, now tragic, and renders a 'service' by arousing the moral and aesthetic sentiments of the public. He produces not only text-books on criminal law, the criminal law itself, and thus legislators, but also art, literature, novels and the tragic drama ... The criminal interrupts the monotony and security of bourgeois life. Thus he protects it from stagnation and brings forth that restless tension, that mobility of spirit without which the stimulus of competition would itself be blunted.[29]

The transition from the social management to the penal treatment of the disorders induced by the fragmentation of wage labour is indeed eminently productive. First, it has spawned new categories of public perception and state action. Echoing the alleged discovery of 'underclass areas' in the United States, in the closing decade of the century Europe has witnessed the invention of the *'quartier sensible'* in France, the 'sink estate' in the United Kingdom, the *'Problemquartier'* in Germany, the *'krottenwijk'* in the Netherlands, etc. – all so many bureaucratic euphemisms to designate the nether sections of the city turned into a social and economic fallow by the state, and for that very reason subjected to reinforced police oversight and correctional penetration.[30] The same goes with the bureaucratic notion of '*violences urbaines*' (plural), coined in France by the Minister of the Interior to amalgamate offensive behaviours of widely divergent natures and motives – mean looks and rude language, graffiti and low-grade vandalism, vehicle theft for joy-riding, brawls between youths, threats to teachers, drug-dealing, and collective confrontations with the police – so as to promote a punitive approach to the social problems besetting declining working-class districts by depoliticising them.

New social types are another by-product of the emerging social-insecurity regime: the irruption of 'superpredators' in the United States, 'feral youth' and 'yobs' in the United Kingdom, or '*sauvageons*' (wildings, a social-paternalistic variant of a racial insult scoffing at the alleged deculturation of the lower classes) in France has been used to justify the reopening or the expansion of detention centres for juveniles, even though all existing studies deplore their noxious effects. To these can be added the renovation of classic types such as the 'career recidivist', the latest avatar of the *uomo delinquente* invented in 1884 by Cesare Lombroso, whose distinctive psychophysiological and anthropometric characteristics are now being researched by experts in criminal 'profiling' as well as guiding the gigantic bureaucratic-cum-scholarly enterprise of 'risk assessment' for the release of sensitive categories of inmates.[31]

For the policy of penalisation of social insecurity is also the bearer of new knowledges about the city and its troubles, broadcast by an unprecedented range of 'experts' and, in their wake, journalists, bureaucrats, the managers of activist organisations, and elected officials perched at the bedside of the 'neighbourhoods of all dangers'.[32] These alleged facts and specialist discourses about criminal inse-curity are given form and put into wide circulation by hybrid institutions, situated at the intersection of the bureaucratic, academic and journalistic fields, which ape research to provide the appearance of a scientific warrant for lowering the police and penal boom on neighbourhoods of relegation. Such is the case, in France, with the Institut des hautes études de la sécurité intérieure, an agency created by the Socialist Minister of the Interior Pierre Joxe in 1989 and then developed by his neo-Gaullist successor Charles Pasqua. This institute, 'placed under the direct authority of the Minister of the Interior' in order to promote 'rational thinking about domestic security', irrigates the country with the latest novelties in 'crime control' imported from America.[33] It is assisted in this enterprise by the Institut de criminologie de Paris, an outfit of law-and-order propaganda which is remarkable for not including a single criminologist among its distinguished members.

It would take pages to list the full roster of the agents and devices that contribute to the collective work of *material and symbolic construction of the penal state* hence-forth charged with reestablishing the state's grip over the populations pushed into the cracks and the ditches of urban space, from private firms of 'safety consultants' to 'adjoints de sécurité' (assistant police officers entrusted with police chores outside of law enforcement), publishing houses eager to peddle books on this hot topic, 'citoyens relais' (volunteers who anonymously tip the police about law-enforcement problems in their neighbourhoods), and a whole series of judicial innovations (adjunct community judges, neighbourhood 'houses of justice', plea bargaining, etc.), which, on the pretext of bureaucratic efficiency, establish a differential justice according to class and place of residence. In sum, *the penalisation of precariousness creates new realities*, and realities tailor-made to legitimise the extension of the prerogatives of the punitive state according to the principle of the self-fulfilling prophecy.

A brief illustration: by treating jostling in the school corridors, rudeness in the classroom or a playground ruckus not as matters of discipline pertaining to pedagogical authority in the establishment but as infractions of the law that must be tallied and centrally compiled via a dedicated computer software (the Signa program) and systematically reported to the local police or magistrates; and by assigning a 'police correspondent' ('*officier référent*') to every secondary school (rather than a psychologist, nurse or social worker, who are direly lacking in lower-class districts), the French authorities have redefined ordinary school troubles as matters of law and order and fabricated an epidemic of 'school violence', even as surveys of students consistently show that over 90 per cent of them feel completely safe at school. With the help of mass media amplification, this 'explosion' of violence serves in turn to justify the 'school-police partnership' that produced it in the first place, and it validates the enrolment of teaching staff in the declining neighbourhoods of the urban periphery in the police missions of surveillance and punishment. Besides, the staging of 'school violence' allows state managers to avoid confronting the professional devaluation and bureaucratic dilemmas created within the educational sphere by the near-universalisation of access to secondary schooling, the growing submission of the school system to the logic of competition, and the imperatives of the 'culture of results' imported from the corporate world.[34]

To understand the fate of the precarious fractions of the working class in their relation to the state, it is no longer possible to limit oneself to studying welfare programmes. The sociology of traditional policies of collective 'well-being' – assistance to dispossessed individuals and households, but also education, housing, public health, family allowances, income redistribution, etc. – must be extended to include penal policies. Thus the study of incarceration ceases to be the reserved province of criminologists and penologists to become an *essential chapter in the sociology of the state and social stratification, and, more specifically, of the (de)composition of the urban proletariat* in the era of ascendant neoliberalism. Indeed, the crystallisation of a liberal-paternalist political regime, which practices '*laisser-faire et laisser-passer*' towards the top of the class structure, at the level of the mechanisms of production of inequality, and punitive paternalism towards the bottom, at the level of their social and spatial implications, demands that we forsake the traditional definition of 'social welfare' as the product of a political and scholarly common sense overtaken by historical reality. It requires that we adopt an expansive approach encompassing in a single grasp the totality of the actions whereby the state purports to mould, classify and control the populations, deemed deviant, dependent and dangerous, living on its territory.

Linking social and penal policies resolves what would appear to be a doctrinal contradiction, or at least a practical antinomy, of neoliberalism, between the downsizing of public authority on the economic flank and its upsizing on that of the enforcement of social and moral order. If the same who are demanding a minimal state in order to 'free' the 'creative forces' of the market and submit the most dispossessed to the sting of competition do not hesitate to erect a maximal state to ensure everyday 'security', it is because *the poverty of the social state against the backdrop of deregulation elicits and necessitates the grandeur of the penal state*. And it is because this causal and functional linkage between the two sectors of the bureaucratic field gets all the stronger, as the state more completely sheds all economic responsibility and tolerates a high level of poverty as well as a wide opening of the compass of inequality.

Probing the use and abuse of incarceration in advanced society at century's dawn reveals that, far from being abnormal deviations or teratological developments retarding the promised advent of 'small government', restrictive workfare and expansive prisonfare are two constituent elements of the neoliberal state. Correspondingly, the struggle for social justice and criminal justice are now enjoined. Activists and researchers who work on the penal front must ally with their counterparts battling on the social front, encompassing both work and welfare, and this on the European level so as to optimise the intellectual and practical resources to be invested in this struggle. For the true alternative to the drift towards the penalisation, soft or hard, of poverty is the construction of a European social state worthy of the name. Today as in the era of its birth, the best means of making the prison recede is to bolster and expand social and economic rights.

Notes

1 The first book, *Punishing the Poor: The Neoliberal Government of Social Insecurity* (Durham and London: Duke University Press, 2009), charts the invention by the United States of a new government of social insecurity wedding restrictive 'workfare' and expansive 'prisonfare'. The second, *Deadly Symbiosis: Race and the Rise of the Penal State* (Cambridge: Polity Press, 2010), plumbs the role of ethnoracial division in accelerating and intensifying the penalisation of urban marginality in the US, Western European and

Brazilian metropolis. The third tome, *Prisons of Poverty*, expanded English edition (Minneapolis: University of Minnesota Press, 2009; first published as *Les Prisons de la misère*, Paris: Raisons d'agir Editions, 1999), tracks the diffusion of US-incubated 'zero-tolerance' policing and related punitive measures across the First and Second worlds as part of the international spread of neoliberalism. This text draws in particular on the Prologue and chapters 1 and 8 of *Punishing the Poor*.

2 Loïc Wacquant, 'La prison est une institution hors-la-loi', *R de réel* 3 (May 2000).

3 For an overview of the penal scene in the main countries of the First World, see John Pratt, Wayne Morrison and Simon Hallsworth (eds), *The New Punitiveness: Trends, Theories, and Perspectives* (London: Willan, 2004); Laurent Mucchielli and Philippe Robert (eds), *Crime et sécurité: l'état des savoirs* (Paris: La Découverte, 2002); Alessandro Dal Lago, *Giovani, stranieri e criminali* (Rome: Manifestolibri, 2001); and Wolfgang Ludwig-Mayerhofer (ed.), *Soziale Ungleichheit, Kriminalität und Kriminalisierung* (Opladen: Leske & Budrich, 2000).

4 I retraced in *Les Prisons de la misère* (see note 1) the three stages in the planetary diffusion of the notions, technologies and policies of public safety 'made in USA': gestation and implementation (as well as exhibition) in New York City under the tutelage of the neoconservative think-tanks that led the campaign against the welfare state; import-export through the agency of the media and of the kindred policy centres that have mushroomed throughout Europe, particularly in Great Britain, which functions as the acclimation chamber of neoliberal penality with a view towards its dissemination on the continent; and scholarly 'dressing up' by local *passeurs* who bring the warrant of their academic authority to the adaptation to their countries of theories and techniques of order maintenance that come from the United States.

5 Robert Castel, *Les Métamorphoses de la question sociale: une chronique du salariat* (Paris: Fayard, 1995); Hartmut Häußermann, Martin Kronauer and Walter Siebel (eds), *An den Rändern der Städte: Armut und Ausgrenzung* (Frankfurt-am-Main: Suhrkamp, 2004); and Loïc Wacquant, *Urban Outcasts: A Comparative Sociology of Advanced Marginality* (Cambridge: Polity Press, 2008).

6 See, in particular, Karl Marx and Friedrich Engels, 'Marx and Engels on crime and punishment', in David Greenberg (ed.), *Crime and Capitalism: Readings in Marxist Criminology* (Palo Alto: Mayfield, 1981); Stephen Lukes and Andrew Scull (eds), *Durkheim and the Law* (Stanford: Stanford University Press, 1995); and Pierre Bourdieu, 'Rethinking the state: on the genesis and structure of the bureaucratic field', in *Practical Reason: On the Theory of Action* (Cambridge: Polity Press, 1998, originally 1994).

7 A forceful argument for recognising the full 'complexity of structure and density of meaning' of punishment as a multilayered social institution, that skilfully draws on Marx, Durkheim, Elias and Foucault, is deployed by David Garland, *Punishment and Society: A Study in Social Theory* (Chicago: University of Chicago Press, 1990), especially at pp. 280–92.

8 Norwegian criminologist Thomas Mathiesen detected and denounced it as early as 1990 on the carceral front; see Thomas Mathiesen, *Prison on Trial: A Critical Assessment* (London: Sage, 1990), pp. 11–14.

9 For an analysis of national variations on this common pattern, read Marion Fourcade-Gourinchas and Sarah L. Babb, 'The rebirth of the liberal creed: paths to neoliberalism in four countries', *American Journal of Sociology* 108 (2002).

10 See Jamie Peck, *Workfare States* (New York: Guilford, 2001), and Catherine Lévy, *Vivre au minimum: enquête dans l'Europe de la précarité* (Paris: Editions La Dispute, 2003).

11 Mike Hawkins, *Social Darwinism in European and American Thought, 1860–1945: Nature as Model and Nature as Threat* (Cambridge: Cambridge University Press, 1997).

12 Pierre Bourdieu *et al.*, *The Weight of the World* (Cambridge: Polity Press, 1999, originally 1993), and Pierre Bourdieu, *Acts of Resistance: Against the Tyranny of the Market* (Cambridge: Polity Press, 1999).

13 In the mid-1970s, the three leading revisionist historians of the prison, David Rothman, Michel Foucault and Michael Ignatieff, agreed to see it as an institution in inevitable decline, destined to be replaced in the medium run by more diffuse, discrete and diversified instruments of social control; see Franklin E. Zimring and Gordon Hawkins, *The Scale of Imprisonment* (Chicago: University of Chicago Press, 1991, chapter 2). The penal debate then turned on the implications of 'decarceration' and implementation of community sentences. Since this Malthusian prognosis, the evolution of punishment has made an about-face in almost all Western societies: the population behind bars has doubled in France, Belgium and England; it has tripled in Holland, Spain and Greece; and it has quintupled in the United States.

14 Clinton's embrace of traditionally republican nostrums on crime is discussed by Ann Chih Lin, 'The troubled success of crime policy', in Margaret Weir (ed.), *The Social Divide: Political Parties and the Future of Activist Government* (Washington, DC: Brookings Institution and Russell Sage Foundation, 1998); on the punitive turn of Blair's New Labour, product of a servile imitation of US policies, read Michael Tonry, *Punishment and Politics: Evidence and Emulation in the Making of English Crime Control Policy* (London: Willan, 2004); the *aggiornamento* of the Italian Left in penal matters is described by Salvatore Verde, *Massima sicurezza: dal carcere speciale allo stato penale* (Rome: Odradek, 2002); the law-and-order conversion of the neo-socialists under Jospin's leadership in France is retraced in Wacquant, *Prisons of Poverty*, part 1 (see note 1).

15 Michel Foucault, 'Du gouvernement des vivants', in *Résumé des cours, 1970–1982* (Paris: Juillard, 1989), my translation. For a historiographic illustration of this notion, read Giovanna Procacci, *Gouverner la misère: la question sociale en France, 1789–1848* (Paris: Seuil, 1993); for a conceptual reconsideration and elaboration, see Nikolas Rose and Mariana Valverde, 'Governed by law?', *Social & Legal Studies* 7:4 (1998).

16 Michael K. Brown, *Race, Money, and the American Welfare State* (Ithaca: Cornell University Press, 1999).

17 Loïc Wacquant, 'Deadly symbiosis: when ghetto and prison meet and mesh', *Punishment & Society* 3:1 (2001).

18 Frances Fox Piven and Richard A. Cloward, *Regulating the Poor: The Functions of Public Welfare*, new expanded edn (New York: Vintage, 1993, originally 1971), xvii.

19 The Gordian knot of racial division and penality in the United States after the peaking of the Civil Rights movement is untied in my book *Deadly Symbiosis* (see note 1). For a preliminary formulation, see Wacquant, 'Deadly symbiosis', as at note 17.

20 Similarities in the culture and organisation of the supervision of single mothers who received public aid and convicts behind bars or released on parole are immediately apparent upon the parallel reading of Sharon Hays, *Flat Broke With Children: Women in the Age of Welfare Reform* (Oxford: Oxford University Press, 2003), and John Irwin, *The Warehouse Prison* (Los Angeles: Roxbury, 2004).

21 See Ann Orloff, 'Gender in the welfare state', *Annual Review of Sociology* 22 (1996), and Julia Adams and Tasleem Padamsee, 'Signs and regimes: reading feminist research on welfare states', *Social Politics* 8:1 (2001).

22 Dorothy Roberts, 'Welfare and the problem of black citizenship', *Yale Law Journal* 105:6 (1996).

23 Loïc Wacquant, 'The penalisation of poverty and the rise of neoliberalism', *European Journal of Criminal Policy and Research*, special issue on 'Criminal justice and social policy', 9:4 (2001); and Tim Newburn and Richard Sparks (eds), *Criminal Justice and Political Cultures: National and International Dimensions of Crime Control* (London: Willan, 2004).

24 Vivien Stern, 'Mass incarceration: "a sin against the future"?', *European Journal of Criminal Policy and Research* 3 (1996), p. 14.

25 David Downes and René van Swaaningen, 'The road to dystopia? Changes in the penal climate of the Netherlands', in Michael Tonry and Catrien Bijleveld (eds), *Crime and Justice in the Netherlands* (Chicago: The University of Chicago Press, 2006).

26 For a critique of the 'demonic myth of the "prison-industrial complex"' in the United States, read Loïc Wacquant, 'The new missions, of the prison in the neoliberal age', in Willem Schinkel (ed.), *Globalization and the State: Sociological Perspectives on the State of the State* (Basingstoke: Palgrave, 2009).

27 'One of the principles of sociology consists in recusing this negative functionalism: social mechanisms are not the product of a Machiavellian intention. They are much more intelligent than the most intelligent of the dominant.' Pierre Bourdieu, *Sociology in Question* (London: Sage, 1990), p. 71, my translation.

28 Michel Foucault, 'Two lectures' (1976), in *Power/Knowledge: Selected Interviews and Other Writings, 1972–1977*, Colin Gordon (ed.) (New York: Pantheon, 1980), p. 97.

29 Karl Marx, *Theories of Surplus Value*, cited in Tom Bottomore and Maximilien Rubel (eds), *Karl Marx: Selected Writings in Society and Social Philosophy* (New York: McGraw-Hill, 1958), p. 159.

30 Loïc Wacquant, *Urban Outcasts: A Comparative Sociology of Advanced Marginality* (London: Polity Press, 2008).

31 The 'power-knowledge' constellation that subtends the genesis and success of the biological theory of crime (then and now) is explored by David Horn in *The Criminal Body: Lombroso and the Anatomy of Deviance* (New York: Routledge, 2003).

32 To recall the savourous expression of one of the French prophets of law-and-order doom, former police commissioner Richard Bousquet, author of *Insécurité: nouveaux risques. Les quartiers de tous les dangers* (Paris: L'Harmattan, 1998).

33 In July of 2004, the IHESI was replaced by the INHES (Institut national des hautes études de sécurité), a very similar outfit presented by then Interior Minister Nicolas Sarkozy as 'the elite school of security that France needs'. Its board of overseers features not a

single researcher. Its work is complemented by the activities of the Observatory on Crime and Delinquency, created by Sarkozy and directed by Alain Bauer, self-proclaimed 'criminologist' and president of Alain Bauer Associates, France's leading consulting firm on 'urban security'.

34 Eric Debardieux, 'Insécurité et clivages sociaux: l'exemple des violences scolaires', *Les Annales de la recherche urbaine* 75 (1997); and Franck Poupeau, *Contestations scolaires et ordre social: les enseignants de Seine-Saint-Denis en grève* (Paris: Syllepse, 2004).

4a Ian Loader

Journeying into, and away from, neoliberal penality[1]

It is by now well known that the USA has for some years been engaged in an unprecedented experiment in mass incarceration whose numerical scale, and human costs, are of staggering proportions. Lower down the slopes of penal expansion, prison numbers in England and Wales have risen to record levels and both main political parties are busy planning further carceral 'investment'. In several other European societies – but importantly, as we shall see, not in all of them – the turn towards penal confinement is also apparent and inmate numbers swell. The prison today looms large in the political and social imagination.

In a series of interventions, of which his Oxford Amnesty Lecture is but one, Loïc Wacquant has in recent years developed an incisive and invaluable analysis of the rise and effects of what he calls the penal state.[2] If he and it did not exist, it would be necessary to invent them. There is much in the contemporary economic, social and penal condition that properly calls for the kind of analysis he offers. That analysis is bold, bustling with energy and arresting prose, and possessed of clarity of intellectual and moral purpose. It is an account resolutely fixed on the big picture and determined not to be distracted by a scholastic insistence of this or that qualifying detail. It is the kind of scholarship that not only extends and deepens understanding of the present, but also enjoins and moves the reader to do something to change it. It is in short, to recover a now unfashionable word, praxis: knowledge for action. In these various respects, Wacquant has been a pioneering and skilled practitioner of one of the lessons he preaches: that as punishment in general, and imprisonment in particular, becomes a structuring institution of social relations and political authority, so its study can no longer be left to penological specialists, but demands the full attention of sociology and political science. It is a telling sign of the times that this call is being heeded.[3]

I shall in this brief response indicate what I think is especially valuable about Wacquant's contribution. But I also want to raise one, not inconsequential, query and make a suggestion as to the political inferences one can best draw from his work.

The query takes us, with Wacquant as our tour guide, on a journey *into* the punishing world of neoliberalism. Here part of my task is to draw attention to aspects of that world which Wacquant's guidance helps us see more clearly. Yet I also want to emphasise the uneven, incomplete and contested character of the neoliberal project; matters that Wacquant's analysis tends to disregard or reduce to 'national inflections' of, and 'institutional variations' upon, the broad transformations that concern him. I do so not, I hope, out of some quibbling fixation with detail and difference, but because these issues matter in helping us determine how vice-like is the grip and reach of neoliberalism's carceral obsession, and how one might best intervene to loosen or contain it. My suggestion speaks to Wacquant's potential value as a guide on a poorly mapped and yet to be taken journey, one navigating a course *away* from neoliberal penality. Wacquant says only a little along these lines in his essay, though he has elsewhere repeatedly stressed that the penal state is 'not destiny' and made scattered remarks about what needs to be done to roll it back.[4] Taking these remarks as my point of departure, I want to think about the intellectual moves that one might today make, as a supplement to the social critique Wacquant offers, in a bid to counter and transcend the ruling penal imaginary.

The journey into neoliberal penality

Wacquant's central claim is that there exists an intimate link between the rise of neoliberal ideology and practice, with its governing ethos of the 'free market' and 'individual responsibility', and the punitive turn taken by the US and several other Western societies over recent decades.[5] Neoliberal rule has entailed a threefold re-articulation of the state's mission: it takes a giant step back from its once active role in the management of the economy; it wholly or partly withdraws the hand of social support; and it extends the reach and intensity of police and penal power. There results a switch from the social to the penal regulation of the poor, jobless and marginal as the prison, not so long ago treated as a failed and waning institution, 'returns to the forefront of the societal stage' – its purpose in a world of insecure employment to discipline and contain the precarious poor and renew the authority of the state. These processes, Wacquant argues, are most developed in the place in which they were forged for home consumption and then for export, the USA. But Europe too is now finding its own path towards the penal government of social insecurity.

What makes Wacquant a useful guide on any journey into the world of neoliberal penality is his highlighting of things that what one may call penal common sense – the taken-for-granted 'truths' about punishment that circulate daily in media and political chatter – either effaces or denies. Four of these are worthy of brief note.

Wacquant's analysis reminds us, firstly, of the inadequacy of any explanation of penal trends which treats them – as penal common sense does – as a response to crime.

Wacquant points out that in the USA the move to lock up in excess of two million citizens has coincided with first flat-lining and then falling crime levels. Mass incarceration may have had a minor part to play in the US crime drop, as some recent analysis has suggested.[6] But any such linkage runs up against societies where crime has fallen since the early 1990s while imprisonment rates remained stable or dipped, such as Canada.[7] Wacquant's point, moreover, is that penal practice is not driven, or is at any rate hugely underdetermined, by patterns of criminal activity. There is a great deal more 'going on' when societies determine who, how and how much to punish, and any convincing account of the rise and scale of incarceration must break with the crime-punishment couplet and look elsewhere.

In his effort to look 'elsewhere', Wacquant reminds us, secondly, that punishment is a mode of regulation, one among a choice of techniques and institutions for governing conduct. Having thereby broken with penal orthodoxy about the obviousness of punishment, he makes clear that neoliberalism has *opted* for penal over social regulation. The 'freeing' of markets, and the eclipse of state-organised social solidarity, produce generalised economic precariousness and insecurity with dual effects. They give rise to a 'martial discourse' that reduces 'security', and the state's role in fostering it, 'to the narrow issue of physical or criminal insecurity', while conjuring up new 'castaway categories' from whom the 'law-abiding' have to be – and demand to be – protected.[8] And they relocate the task of regulating the poor from welfare to penal agencies, such that it now unfolds, as Wacquant eloquently puts it, in 'stern scenarios in police stations, in the corridors of criminal courts, and in the darkness of prison cells'. The result is the frenzied proliferation of offences, orders, penalties, surveillance technology and governmental activity and innovation that has in recent years been spawned by the criminal question.

Wacquant recalls, thirdly, that incarceration is not merely a set of repressive institutions and practices devoted to the exclusion, control, confinement, containment and banishment of 'dispossessed and dishonoured populations' – matters that have long been the stock-in-trade of materialist criminology. Punishment is also, and at the same time, productive. It generates and circulates classifications and categories, ways of thinking and feeling, lines of vision and division; it sends authoritative signals about political authority, moral boundaries, the nature of power, about who does and who doesn't belong.[9] Wacquant's particular point here is that the advent of penal management of the poor has given rise to new 'social types' and categories that permeate public consciousness and shape thought and action – predators, feral youths, sink estates, ASBOs, asylum seekers, etc. But this, more generally, forces us to rethink how we conceive of the police, courts and prisons which are today, Wacquant argues, not only instruments of control but 'a core political capacity through which the state both produces and manages inequality, identity and marginality'.[10]

Finally, Wacquant unsettles what risks becoming a complacent and self-satisfied (European) assumption that when it comes to incarceration the USA stands in a category of its own. To be sure, a glance at the International Centre for Prison Studies' World Prison Brief lends some support to this view, or at least indicates a gulf in penal practice between the US and Western Europe.[11] Wacquant's rejoinder is three-pronged. First, he traces the efforts of New Right think-tanks, police chiefs and other policy entrepreneurs to export neoliberal penality to Europe – with England and Wales acting as an 'acclimatization chamber'.[12] Second, he points to what he argues is the hyperincarceration of migrants and foreign nationals in Europe's prisons, a measure by which European penal systems look more severe and discriminatory than the USA's.[13] Thirdly, Wacquant contends that a 'European road' to the penal state is taking shape – with different national inflections in, for example, France, Italy and the Netherlands. This, he contends, involves a meshing of welfare and justice interventions and an 'ever more precise and penetrating' police surveillance, rather than simply penal confinement, of minority and marginal populations – what Wacquant terms social panopticism.

This is a useful corrective to any overly 'othering' depiction (by Europeans) of the gap between carceral practices in Europe and the USA – one that also helpfully reminds us not to make imprisonment rates the sole indicator of penal severity.[14] However, it is at this point that my query arises. It concerns Wacquant's portrayal of the reach and grip of neoliberal penality.

My doubts in respect of reach are prompted by the resistance of some societies to the export of neoliberal penality and the persistence of alternative ways of thinking and acting in respect of punishment and its relation to society. On the export point, Wacquant tends to conflate the presence of activity, which he and others have documented a great deal, with its success, when the evidence suggests that elements of neoliberal penality – zero tolerance, for example – have not 'travelled' well.[15] 'The grand American experiment of the "War on Crime"' has simply not been a 'mandatory reference for the governments of the First World', as Wacquant claims. It has repulsed and repelled, as well as seduced and attracted. We need, in addition, to record the variation in penal practice that is still to be found across Western states, and the persistence of societies that have managed to create or sustain relatively mild penal systems. Though it has made other moves towards the penal regulation of the poor in recent years, it nonetheless remains the case that imprisonment rates in France have remained stable over the last decade. More tellingly, Canada has cut prison numbers by 11 per cent since 1997 with policies in marked and conscious contrast to those pursued in neighbouring USA. Finland has in recent years radically cut its prison population and actively strives to keep the scale and temper of punishment within 'Scandinavian' norms. Norway has long sustained a relatively benign penal culture, as has Germany.[16] There is, of course, room for legitimate debate about the significance of these differences and about how to weigh imprisonment rates against other measures of penal harshness or mildness. But they offer reasons to remain sceptical of any account which suggests that international penal practice is resolutely following a single – neoliberal – trajectory.[17]

We might ask, secondly, about the hold that neoliberal penality has in those places where it appears hegemonic. It is certainly true, as Wacquant points out, that punitive policies have been the object of 'an unprecedented political consensus' over the last decade or so. It is arguably less clear, however, that they 'enjoy broad public support'. This is partly a question of how one interprets that noisy, vocal and superficially punitive public clamour which does exist – as unremittingly hostile towards criminal scapegoats, or, as has been suggested, as one of the few legitimate outlets for citizens of a neoliberal polity to express solidarity with strangers, in this case with crime victims.[18] There is also much documented evidence of lay ambivalence towards punishment[19] – sufficient to warrant the claim that punitive policies are the result less of overwhelming popular demand than of the wilful or risk-averse misreading of 'public opinion' by rulers convinced that political responsibility means uncritically translating whatever mass mediated voices press most forcefully upon them. To this one might add that penal practice has not been all-of-a-piece even within neoliberal heartlands, with significant variation to be found among US states as well as between England and Wales and Scotland.[20] And one can point to the continued professional contestation of neoliberal penal policies and the attendant survival and revival of forms of rehabilitation,[21] as well as to penal reform groups whose campaigns continue to monitor and expose the excesses of neoliberal penality and mobilise around alternative programmes such as restorative conferencing or 'justice reinvestment'.

Why does all this matter? Not because it detracts from the persuasive force of Wacquant's argument, the main contours of which I do not dispute.[22] But because this unevenness provides a reminder that neoliberal penality remains an insecure and contested ideology not a political movement that has swept all before it and crushed competing social visions underfoot. There remain places one can learn from, and forces and ideas that prefigure alternative futures.

A journey away from neoliberal penality?

Wacquant has, it should be noted, given some attention to questions of resistance and alternatives. He argues, both in this text and elsewhere, that the penal state is not a 'foregone conclusion', in Europe at least. He has called for 'words and discourses' that expose penal common sense to 'rigorous logical and empirical critique'; for 'judicial policies and practices' that thwart the extension of the penal and police dragnet and encourage 'a social, health or educational alternative whenever feasible'; and for coalitions of activists in the penal and social fields. To make prison 'recede', he contends, one must 'strengthen and expand social and economic rights'.[23]

There is nothing in these suggestions that I disagree with. Yet the question of how to disrupt the logic of incarceration, and set out alternatives that do more than nostalgically seek to breathe new life into penal-welfarism, remains underspecified, in Wacquant's work and elsewhere in recent writings on punishment.[24] As a result, the journey *away* from neoliberal penality comes with few detailed maps, making it easy to lose one's way. It is also attended by no shortage of hostility. From the Right, the owners, cheerleaders and beneficiaries of what Wacquant calls the 'law-and-order merry-go-round' disqualify such thinking as the acts of a 'vain dreamer' or of ideologues ignorant of the 'harsh realities of contemporary urban life' and willing to play fast and loose with the safety of their co-citizens. But such thinking also attracts scorn from many on the Left who dismiss it as the wishful utopianism of those divorced from material realities and practical struggle. Such activity is not for them: it is time for another dystopian trot around the track marked social critique.[25]

Yet there is a danger here of the liberal-left missing an opportunity – one opened up by the 2008 financial crash and the ensuing global recession – to offer an alternative reading of the intersection between neoliberal excess and the turn to incarceration.[26] There is a conventional account of the relationship between recession, crime and punishment which would predict, in the wake of the financial crisis, a further tightening of the penal screw. The claim here is that punitive policies have over the last decade coincided with falling levels of volume crime; so imagine how much more severe things will become when crime rates rise and governments come under renewed pressure to 'crack down' from the media, victims groups and opinion polls, or else sense a political opportunity to deploy crime in the upkeep of their battered legitimacy. As recession bites, economic precariousness deepens and social tension mounts, one should anticipate the entrenchment and extension of the penal government of poverty. There are, in other words, many reasons of a Wacquantian sort for thinking we are about to journey further into the world of neoliberal penality, not away from it.

It may be possible, however, to tell another story, one that draws a different inference from Wacquant's analysis and seeks to reorder understanding of neoliberal penality in ways that supply new grounds for moving beyond it. This account runs something like this. The 'credit crunch' has exposed the excesses of a lightly regulated global banking system. It is now apparent that during years of economic growth – at which time they were worshipped and celebrated – bankers took decisions for short-term gain in disregard of the adverse effects of their actions upon others and the long-term costs of their reckless behaviour. The unregulated market has, once again, eaten itself. In the wake of the global governmental intervention that is desperately trying to avert financial meltdown, it appears that the Thatcher-Reagan inspired era of neoliberal excess is exhausted and we are at the dawn of a new age of regulated responsibility. This much is now familiar. But why stop there? Can we not apply this analysis to other domains of public life and in particular to penal policy? Is reckless excess not also an accurate description of how in recent decades successive US and British governments have responded to crime and used punishment: for short-term political advantage, with scant attention to the collateral consequences of, say, mass imprisonment, and in careless disregard of the long-term effects of their policies? Might this therefore, by extension, be an appropriate moment to take stock of where three decades of neoliberal penality has left us; to reflect on the trajectory, temper and impact of punitive penal policies; and to contemplate a different course?[27]

Economic recession may, for these reasons, offer an unlikely but nonetheless potent opportunity for generating a new public discourse about neoliberal penality and why and how to break from it. It may act as a spur for people to consider seriously 'the question of [prison's] financial burden, social costs and civic implications' – a question, Wacquant points out, that has been politically off-limits during neoliberalism's ascendency. That question may now be pressed by those with a Treasury mindset who are no longer willing or able to bear the monetary and fiscal price of a society's prison binge. But it also requires, of those who research, think, write and campaign in the field of punishment, a re-posing of some old questions, not only about the purpose, but first and foremost about the 'scale of imprisonment'.[28] This, in turn, calls for exploration of the value and purchase of a public philosophy organised around ideas of restraint, parsimony and dignity – one that breaks decisively with the fantasy that punishment can deliver decent, secure societies. We have been witness – with Loïc Wacquant's considerable help – to the immense social costs of neoliberalism's penal experiment. It is time to recover the social meanings, and practice the political art, of penal moderation.

Notes

1 Editor's note: Ian Loader acted as respondent to Loïc Wacquant's Oxford Amnesty Lecture in February 2007, but he wrote this response to Wacquant's text in February 2009.

2 Most recently in Loïc Wacquant, *Punishing the Poor: The Neoliberal Government of Social Insecurity* (Durham and London: Duke University Press, 2009). Interested readers might also usefully consult *Prisons of Poverty*, expanded English edition (Minneapolis: University of Minnesota Press, 2009); 'Deadly symbiosis: when ghetto and prison meet and mesh', *Punishment & Society* 3:1 (2001); and 'Penalization, depoliticization, racialization: on the over-incarceration of immigrants in the European Union', in S. Armstrong and L. McAra (eds), *Perspectives on Punishment: The Contours of Control* (Oxford: Oxford University Press, 2009). For a sympathetic, but critical, assessment of Wacquant's work on penality, see chapter 5 of Tom Daems, *Making Sense of Penal Change* (Oxford: Oxford University Press, 2008).

3 See, for example, Bruce Western, *Punishment and Inequality in America* (New York: Russell Sage, 2006); Devah Pager, *Marked: Race, Crime, and Finding Work in an Era of Mass*

Incarceration (Chicago: Chicago University Press, 2007); and Lisa Miller, *The Perils of Federalism: Race, Poverty and the Politics of Crime Control* (Oxford: Oxford University Press, 2008).

4 See, for example, Loïc Wacquant, 'The advent of the penal state is not destiny', *Social Justice* 28:3 (2001) and 'The penalisation of poverty and the rise of neoliberalism', *European Journal of Criminal Policy and Research* 9 (2001).

5 Wacquant is by no means alone is making neoliberalism the villain of the piece when explaining recent trends in punishment and crime control. See also Alessandro de Giorgi, *Re-thinking the Political Economy of Punishment: Perspectives on Post-Fordism and Penal Policy* (Aldershot: Ashgate, 2006); Robert Reiner, *Law and Order: The Honest Citizen's Guide to Crime and Control* (Cambridge: Polity, 2007); and Nicola Lacey, *The Prisoners' Dilemma: Political Economy and Punishment in Contemporary Democracies* (Cambridge: Cambridge University Press, 2008).

6 See, for example, Franklin E. Zimring, *The Great American Crime Decline* (Oxford: Oxford University Press, 2007).

7 *Ibid.*, chapter 5.

8 For further analysis of the contemporary political reduction of 'existential insecurity' to 'the apparently straightforward issue of "law and order"', see Zygmunt Bauman, *Globalization: The Human Consequences* (Cambridge: Polity Press, 1998) and *Liquid Fear* (Cambridge: Polity Press, 2006).

9 There has been a rich neo-Durkheimian exploration of these themes within recent sociology of punishment, following the publication of David Garland's *Punishment and Modern Society* (Oxford: Oxford University Press, 1990). See, for example, Philip Smith, *Punishment and Culture* (Chicago: University of Chicago Press, 2008).

10 Cognate analyses of the prominent place that categories of crime and control have come to occupy within the UK and US political system, in workplaces, schools and families, and in the daily routines and thought-behaviour of citizens, can be found in David Garland, *The Culture of Control* (Oxford: Oxford University Press, 2001) and Jonathan Simon, *Governing through Crime* (Oxford: Oxford University Press, 2007).

11 According to recent figures (from the International Centre for Prison Studies' World Prison Brief, www.kcl.ac.uk/depsta/law/research/icps/worldbrief/wpb_stats.php, accessed 13 February 2009) the USA tops the international league table imprisoning 756 per 100,000 of its citizens, followed by the Russian Federation at 629. The highest ranked European Union member is Latvia (ranked 37th at 288 per 100,000) while the highest placed Western European state is Spain (79th at 160 per 100,000) followed by Luxembourg (84th at 155 per 100,000) and England & Wales (88th at 152 per 100,000). Some interpretive caution is required here, however. As several observers have pointed out, prison rates are produced by a range of factors and are not necessarily a reliable indicator of the severity of a penal culture – Congo (Brazzaville), for example, comes next to the bottom of the table with a prison population of 22 per 100,000 citizens. For a discussion of these issues see Michael Tonry, 'Determinants of penal policies', in M. Tonry (ed.), *Crime, Punishment and Politics in Comparative Perspective* (Chicago: Chicago University Press, 2007).

12 See Loïc Wacquant, 'How penal common sense comes to Europeans: notes on the Transatlantic diffusion of neoliberal doxa', *European Societies* 1:3 (1999). On diffusion

of the neoliberal model to South America, see his 'Towards a dictatorship over the poor? notes on the penalization of poverty in Brazil', *Punishment & Society* 5:2 (2003).

13 See his 'Suitable enemies: foreigners and immigrants in Europe's prisons', *Punishment & Society* 1:2 (1999), and 'Penalization, depoliticization, racialization' as in note 2. The World Prison Brief figures on foreign prisoners can be found at www.kcl.ac.uk/depsta/law/research/icps/worldbrief/wpb_stats.php?area=all&category=wb_foreign (accessed 28 February 2009).

14 Despite knowing that they form only part of a broader patchwork of penal regulation, criminologists still tend to fixate on prison numbers as rough shorthand for punitiveness, partly because of the accessibility of relevant figures. It is much to Wacquant's credit that he does not do so.

15 Trevor Jones and Tim Newburn, *Policy Transfer and Criminal Justice* (Maidenhead: Open University Press, 2006).

16 See the contributions collected in Tonry (ed.), *Crime, Punishment and Politics* as in note 11.

17 For a thoughtful discussion of the issues raised here, see Richard Sparks, 'Degrees of estrangement: the cultural theory of risk and comparative penology', *Theoretical Criminology* 5:2 (2001).

18 Richard Sparks, '"Bringin' it all back home": populism, media coverage and the dynamics of locality and globality in the politics of crime control', in Kevin Stenson and Robert Sullivan (eds), *Crime, Risk and Justice* (Cullompton, Devon: Willan, 2000).

19 See, among others, Julian Roberts and Mike Hough Roberts, *Understanding Public Attitudes to Criminal Justice* (Maidenhead: Open University Press, 2005); Neil Hutton, 'Beyond populist punitiveness?', *Punishment & Society* 7:3 (2005); and Elizabeth K. Brown, 'The dog that did not bark: punitive social views and the "professional middle classes"', *Punishment & Society* 8:3 (2006).

20 On the US, see Vanessa Barker, *The Politics of Imprisonment* (New York: Oxford University Press, 2009); for recent developments in Scotland see *Scotland's Choice: The Report of the Scottish Prisons Commission*, available at www.scotland.gov.uk/Resource/Doc/230180/0062359.pdf (accessed 22 February 2009). The Commission was set up by the minority nationalist administration in Scotland in 2008 with a brief to find an alternative penal course to that being followed in England and Wales.

21 See Gwen Robinson, 'Late-modern rehabilitation: the evolution of a penal strategy', *Punishment & Society* 10:4 (2008).

22 One of the small pleasures of chairing a lecture is that one gets to observe audience reaction – including their bodily demeanour – as the lecture is delivered. I think I detected two archetypal reactions to Wacquant's. The first, which I mention here, is that of an empirical criminologist who keeps a running check of the details ignored and rhetorical over-statements uttered and who becomes increasingly irritated as the tally of each mounts. I raise this precisely because that was not my response, nor the impulse behind the reservations I have just expressed.

23 Wacquant, 'The penalisation of poverty' as in note 4.

24 There is, of course, one notable exception – that of restorative justice.

25 This brings me to the second archetypal reaction I think I detected among the audience at Wacquant's lecture. This is that of the left-liberal student, or concerned

citizen, who takes a kind of gloomy, self-reaffirming delight in being instructed by the Berkeley Professor that the world really is as unremittingly grim as they thought it was when they entered the lecture hall. One worries that Wacquant's 'global' analysis of neoliberal penality may have the unintended effect among such listeners of unbending the springs of action.

26 My – pre-financial crash – attempt to sketch the outlines of such a reading can be found in Ian Loader, 'Ice cream and incarceration: on appetites for security and punishment', *Punishment & Society* 11:2 (2009).

27 It is hardly irrelevant here that the US has just inaugurated a new government on the promise of change, investment and inclusion – following an election in which domestic crime and punishment featured hardly at all. It may well be that President Obama has little political or constitutional room to make much of a material difference to America's bloated prison system. He can however alter the political mood music and begin to chip away at dominant penal articulations of the relationship between crime, poverty and punishment.

28 Franklin E. Zimring and Gordon Hawkins, *The Scale of Imprisonment* (Chicago: University of Chicago Press, 1991).

5 Thomas Mathiesen

Ten reasons for not building more prisons[1]

This essay deals with the future of prisons. Should we have more prisons? I think not. Instead, I propose a total ban on prison construction. I have the industrialised, wealthy countries of the West in mind, where there is an economy which makes the construction of new prisons possible, and tempting for governments. In other parts of the world, where the prison issue is just as acute but where there is no such economy, a different medicine will be needed. Let me first point to two types of contextualisation of the question.

Organisational context

Firstly, it is important to point out that in terms of *organisational context*, the position of prisons in the Western world has changed considerably since the 1960s and 1970s. Much more than before, the prison system is solidified by being integrated into a wider context of control measures. Earlier, each of the various agencies dealing with crime had a more or less separate status. Today the border-lines between the different agencies have become much more diffuse. For example, in Norway's prisons, probation, parole and various forms of 'punishment in the community' (*samfunnsstraff*, a recent invention in Norway), are more or less collapsed into one 'service' or system. There is no longer a separate Prison Act, but a general Punishment Act, covering all offenders in various stages of punishment, from remand before trial through closed, medium security and more or less open prisons, to the various forms of punishment in the community. Consequently, staff members of institutions and agencies which earlier were responsible (at least formally) for care and welfare and not punishment of offenders, have now become the executors of punishment by being a part of a punishment chain covering all of the various agencies. Protests from social workers and other professionals have not been able to stop this. Similar trends are also noticeable in other Western countries.

This, however, is not the end of integration in the control field. Policing has also changed, and has become more integrated with the punishment chain. Information floats between the punishment chain and the police. To a larger extent than before, policing today is *future* rather than past oriented (who are the future criminals?), it is *risk* oriented (what is the chance that people commit crime in the future?) and it is *category* oriented (which categories – for example which nationalities – show the greatest risks?). Of course, old fashioned policing – past oriented, tracing specific criminals on an individual basis – certainly still exists, and there is partly resistance in various branches of the police to new technology making future-oriented policing possible, but this is a trend.[2] Information from the agencies in the punishment chain, including the prisons, is therefore of great interest to the police. The trend started before 'the war against terrorism', but was stepped up after 11 September 2001. The threat to civil liberties and human rights is obvious.

In turn, policing of this kind is dependent on modern information technology, which brings the police in contact with the new national and international, even global, surveillance and control systems. I am thinking of the Schengen Information System, SIS, with close to 895 thousand people (in addition to hundreds of thousands of aliases plus more than seventeen million objects) on their central database on a single day in the beginning of 2007.[3] The Schengen Information System is particularly oriented to control of the common EU border. Thus, 84 per cent of the 895 thousand on the Schengen database on a single day in 2007 were 'unwanted aliens', entered pursuant to Article 96 of the Schengen Convention. But there is also a strong orientation towards public policy and public security, including state security, which is a 'core goal' specified as a general purpose in Article 93 of the Convention. On a single day in 2003 there were an estimated 125 thousand access terminals to the Schengen Information System throughout Europe.[4] A technically much more advanced SIS II is in the making.

There are also other systems: I am thinking of the SIRENE exchange of information (the acronym is for Supplementary Information Request at the National Entries). Each of the countries participating in the Schengen Information System has a SIRENE office, responsible for the national administration of SIS. The SIRENE offices may exchange almost any type of auxiliary information about individuals entered on the SIS database with any other SIRENE office in the other Schengen member states. I am, furthermore, thinking of the law enforcement agency Europol, with its three information systems known as TECS, 'the Europol Computer Systems'. There is: a general *information system* where information about individuals is entered; a system of *work files* where over fifty types of more or less sensitive personal information may be entered (under some conditions even information on sexual matters, and political and religious opinion); and an *index system*. I am thinking of the EURODAC fingerprint system ('the European Asylum

System'), where fingerprints and other information about virtually all asylum seekers in Europe is entered and remains there for years. I am thinking of the Directive 2006/24/EC on the retention of communication traffic data, which makes storage of extensive traffic data in connection with the use of telephones (who calls who, when, where etc.), the use of mobiles, e-mail, and the internet, mandatory for months or years. And so on. Details about these systems may be obtained elsewhere. In general the systems in question are being increasingly integrated, while the ties of control 'from below', that is, from the nation states, are being increasingly diluted.[5]

The point here is that the national police of a country, such as Norway, becomes a link to these systems on the one hand, and a link to the broad and inclusive punishment chain, including the prisons, on the other. The 'war against terrorism' after 11 September 2001, which has led to a greatly widened and highly diffuse concept of terrorism,[6] easily including political refugees, asylum seekers, demonstrators at important political events, and so on, has solidified the police function as a link. We may envisage, in the future, a vast and integrated control system with dangerous functions for civil liberties and the rule of law. A development such as this is of course backed by strong political forces, and by the media (especially television) as an agenda-setting institution.

The context of resistance

But I do not want to leave you with the impression that the integration of the prison system into a wider context of control measures is the whole story.

In terms of criticism and protest, the late 1960s and the 1970s are viewed by many today as an incomparably glorious past, with critical political activity on a level we never can reach again. And certainly, many important things happened in the 1970s. In the field of prisons and criminal policy, the development of the prison movement throughout Europe is a case in point.[7] But, important as they were in their time, many of the active and lively organisations established in that period, which were oriented towards abolition and/or change of prisons, no longer exist.[8]

The feeling is that such a time will never come again. This is not true, argues the Swedish sociologist Stellan Vinthagen. Contrasting the bleak story of our own time, there is an alternative story. A story of resistance in our time. Vinthagen forcefully points out that in terms of numbers alone there are probably more people engaged in critical protests today than there were in the 1970s.[9] Look at the anti-globalisation movements. Look at the peace movements. They recruit tens and hundreds of thousands of participants, all over the world. Just think of the world-wide protest in the spring of 2003, just before the United States, Britain and other states illegally – that is, without a UN sanction – invaded Iraq. And that is only one example. There is potential, there is hope, argues Vinthagen.

I think he is right. To be sure, the repressive forces are formidable. The forces – the calls for more police, more prisons, ultimately for more votes to given political parties – are grounded in economic, political and military conditions. But above all, they are media-based. The tabloid newspapers and the equally tabloid television channels, as well as other media, both create and support the calls. The media communicate stories of daily crime, organised crime and terrorism which, though of course realities, are nevertheless grossly exaggerated, sometimes into full scale moral panics, in Western societies. The forces in question have got the diffuse and wide concept of terrorism, mentioned above, as an additional weapon and legitimation of repression of activities far away from terrorism.

But this should not stop us. The potential for criticism, critique and resistance exists. The point is to elicit the potential. There is a good chance that we may be able to channel some of the potential in the direction of penal and control issues. A vast number of anti-globalisation and peace demonstrators have been in touch with the police and the penal system. Take the protest against the EU summit in Gothenburg, Sweden, in June 2001. A large number of demonstrators, who were there just to demonstrate and not to throw bricks and sticks (although bricks and sticks were thrown, of course), were arrested and spent the night in police custody. Many foreigners among them were extradited. They were prevented from exercising their right to demonstrate and their right to free speech. I was in contact with many of the Norwegians who had been handled this way, and we wrote a small book relating their experiences.[10] Of course, they immediately and clearly saw the relevance of penal and criminal policy. A number of people were also brought to trial and given unconditional prison sentences after Gothenburg. The Swedish sentences were extremely long, in some cases a matter of years – and much longer, incidentally, than prison sentences after demonstrations at other summits. Though many sentences were reduced by the Supreme Court, they were still long. In short, the legal system was certainly alerted and activated. The importance of penal and control policy came uncomfortably close for those serving time inside the walls.

So the potential may indeed be channelled towards penal and criminal policy. Now, there are of course varying opinions about prisons, also among people such as demonstrators. A few wish to abolish prisons altogether, others wish to have fewer prisons, still others wish to reform the prisons. There is today hardly a united front as far as this goes among critically minded people, even if they have had unpleasant encounters with the control system.

But many critically minded people who have had such encounters would agree, I think, that at least we do not want *more* prisons. We do not want our prison system to swell further without a clear stop signal. I would propose a *ban on prison-building* as a first core issue around which to build a new prison movement, based on the potential inherent in the post-modern anti-globalisation and peace movements.

In a sense, this is a highly reformist issue. But with time it stands a good chance of evolving into a more fundamentally and broadly critical way of thinking about prisons and the penal system.

Building programmes are on the march on a wide scale in Europe and the United States, thus widening and solidifying the prison solution to the problems at hand. At the same time, there is a whole string of good reasons for *not* building more prisons. Also, there is an absence of good reasons for building more. Regardless of other differences of opinion, a ban on building more prisons is something which it would be fairly easy to get agreement on among critically oriented persons and groups. It is probably even easy, with time, to get agreement on it on a broad political and international scale.

I want now to present ten arguments against building more prisons. Around these arguments, a movement can be created, as I have said, drawing on the potential inherent in today's anti-globalisation and peace movements. I have presented some of the arguments earlier in embryonic form.[11] But that was before the development of the anti-globalisation and peace movements as they are today. Also, I have added more arguments, making a total of ten. I will mention them briefly, one by one. Keep in mind that for each of them, there is an extensive criminological and philosophical literature. Here I am just highlighting the major points.[12] Through the past years or decades of punitive populism, many of the arguments I have in mind have faded into the background. It is important to renew their status as figure rather than just ground in criminological and criminal policy debate.

The ten arguments

Rehabilitative ineffectiveness

First, there is the argument of rehabilitative ineffectiveness. There are now thousands of studies and meta-studies indicating that treatment in a wide sense in prison does not work, or works only to a very small extent. 'Work' here pertains to reduction of recidivism.

Let me be very precise: prisoners are in great need of caring or welfare services. They are generally without money, without employment, without education, without housing, often drug addicts, without good health. I will return to this towards the end of this essay. Moreover, prisoners have a right to such services, partly as ordinary citizens who have a right to health services, education, and so on, and specifically as prisoners, who are under the forced custody of the state, and who are therefore especially entitled to the rights in question. These are inalienable rights, *regardless of the prison's success or failure in terms of recidivism*. Its high degree of failure in terms of recidivism is clear, but that must not be allowed to intervene with the prisoners' obvious human right to a series of services. In other words, it must not allow us to say that because the prison is largely a failure, we might as well lock the gates and throw away the key. Rather than anchoring services in success in terms of recidivism, they must be anchored by law as precisely that: inalienable human rights.

Research and opinion in the area of recidivism have gone through three fairly distinct phases. Increasingly after World War II, and up through the 1960s, an optimistic trend developed. Through psychiatric and related methods, prisoners could presumably be 'cured' of their predilection to engage in crime. A long development in legal and forensic thinking opened for this notion. But few success stories followed. On the contrary, alarming failures were reported.[13] In the 1970s a second phase emerged, which was summarised in slogan form as 'nothing works', an expression coined by the media rather than the researchers. The name of Robert Martinson is firmly tied to this phase. In a review of 231 methodologically sound research studies of treatment programmes in the US and Europe between 1945 and 1967, called the ECT report ('Effectiveness of Correctional Treatment'), he concluded that virtually no effect, in terms of recidivism, could be found when comparisons with control groups were made.[14] In a later article on the subject he conceded that some effects and variations could in fact be discerned (perhaps his methodological demands at that time were somewhat less stringent).[15]

During the 1990s and early 2000s, however, a third phase has been developing. The slogan is no longer 'nothing works', but rather 'what works?' A long string of meta-studies (totalising studies looking for general trends in large numbers of individual studies which satisfy methodological demands) have appeared. The researchers suggest more optimistic results as far as corrections are concerned. The so-called CDATE project and Mark Lipsey's work are cases in point.[16] They are major recent reviews of the research literature. But also these reviews show very modest results, and formulations such as 'the effect size is still rather small', and 'weak or negligible effects on recidivism', are used. For example, though stating that differences found are useful for practice, Mark Lipsey and collaborators make the telling conclusion that

> Though this result supports many different program choices, it should be noted that most of the interventions tested in the research literature produced weak or negligible effects on recidivism, and some had negative effects. Despite the evidence that many programs, in principle, can be effective, actually configuring and imple-menting such a program appears to be relatively difficult.

Bear in mind that the issue here is *whether or not to build more prisons.* Fine if results, though 'weak or negligible', are found in (some) existing prisons. In any case, 'weak or negligible effects' is not an argument for building more prisons. On the contrary, it is a forceful argument for dismantling all major building programmes.[17]

Preventive ineffectiveness

Secondly, there is the argument of preventive ineffectiveness – that is, ineffectiveness in terms of preventing *others*, in the outside community, from committing crime through deterrence, habit formation, moral persuasion and the like. We usually refer to this as general prevention, sometimes just simply deterrence.

General prevention, deterrence of others in the community, is the major argument of at least Norwegian courts when sentences are passed. A person must presumably be given this or that sentence 'for reasons of general prevention'. Note clearly that I am here talking about the preventive effect of *prison*, not of fines, not of parking tickets and all of the other types of formal sanctions (though I think quite a few of the research results are relevant also to non-prison sanctions). And, to repeat once more, I am not drawing conclusions about the very existence of prisons, and not the very existence of a prison system; I am just drawing conclusions about building more prisons.

The results of a large number of research studies, over many years, are bleak. Take Karl Schumann and collaborators' comprehensive sociological study of general prevention among youthful offenders in Germany.[18] Across a wide range of types of youthful crimes, they found no preventive effect. Take Richard Wright's extensive summary of the preventive effect of prison, which, notably, includes the much-debated econometric studies based on economic cost-benefit models.[19] Elsewhere I have summarised Wright,[20] who actually defends the prison, in the following words, to say that as far as general prevention goes, there is:

1 *a moderate relationship between the actual and subjectively expected probability of punishment and criminal behaviour* (that is, as a moderate relationship, the greater the actual and expected risk of being caught and punished, the less inclined you will be to commit crime);

2 *a moderate initial effect on criminal behaviour, but very small long-term effects,* of sudden changes in criminal policy increasing the expected probability of punishment; and

3 *no relationship* between either the actual or the expected severity of punishment and crime.

In simpler terms, research shows that there are perhaps moderate preventive effects of police efficiency in terms of detection abilities.[21] Being caught and consequently punished in some form has a moderate effect. There may perhaps, then, be a 'bottom level' in terms of punishment which you cannot pass without its having an effect on public morality. But we are far from that bottom level, because *there are no effects from the severity of prison sentences.* Sentences may be short, medium or long – there are no effects on prevention of those who are in the outside community. Why? There are probably good normative reasons. Norms and morality keep most people away from crime, at least from ordinary street crime. Some people are in or enter into a situation where norms and moral doubts are more or

less neutralised, either temporarily or for longer periods of time depending on
the context in which they live. They are generally in a situation where the threat
of punishment is also neutralised. The drug addict on the street just has to have
money for his next shot. No threat of punishment in the world can stop him. Perhaps
you could put it this way, in bold relief: the general prevention of punishment
possibly functions in relation to those who do not 'need' it, that is, those who
are law-abiding anyway. In relation to those who 'need' it, that is, those who for
various reasons are prone not to be law-abiding, it does not function (and those
who organise crime behind the scenes, get away anyway).

These results constitute a powerful argument against using stiff(er) prison
sentences, and an argument for lowering sentences. Stiff(er) prison sentences in
turn clog up the facilities and consequently create an irrational call for building
new prisons.[22]

Incapacitative ineffectiveness

Thirdly, there is the question of incapacitation – imprisonment simply in order to
prevent those who are imprisoned from committing new acts while they are inside
the walls, this in order to decrease the crime rate.

There are two major varieties of incapacitation. Firstly, there is so-called
'collective incapacitation', where whole categories of people (for example those
who have been imprisoned twice or three times before) are kept behind bars for
long periods of time or forever. 'Three strikes and you're out', is the saying. The
developments in the United States until the mid-1980s (and beyond, for that matter)
can be viewed as an enormous experiment in collective incapacitation.[23] The Panel
on Research on Criminal Careers, chaired by Alfred Blumstein and sponsored by
the National Institute of Justice, published its major two-volume report in 1986.[24]
The panel paid close attention to the issue of incapacitation. Between 1973 and
1982 the number of state and federal prisoners in the US almost doubled – yet the
crime rate increased by 29 per cent. Estimates available to the panel suggested that
depending on the assumed individual offending frequency, the rate would have been
10 to 20 per cent higher if the almost 100 per cent increase in prison figures had
not occurred. This may be viewed as a modest gain, but certainly an extremely costly
one, in terms of money as well as suffering, in view of the dramatic increase in the
prison population. Most significantly, Blumstein and colleagues report that further
reductions would 'require at least 10 to 20 per cent increases in inmate populations
for each 1 per cent reduction in crime'.[25] In short, only a marginal effect of collective
incapacitation is demonstrated. Despite this, the enormous further increase in
American prison figures has continued into the 2000s. It is a well-known fact
that each year, new babies are born. Each year new generations of young people
consequently commit criminal acts. Nothing is done about that by placing the older
generations in prison. All you get is a swelling prison population: according to the

logic of collective incapacitation, you have to go on keeping the older generations behind bars while you admit the new ones, until you get staggering prison populations. This is exactly what happened in the United States.

Secondly, there is 'selective incapacitation'. The difference between collective and selective incapacitation is actually a matter of degree. The salient point is this: rather than imprisoning whole groups or categories of offenders, attempts have been made to predict which individuals are most likely to recidivate, especially to serious crimes. Selective incapacitation has a long story, and represents several serious issues.[26] I shall only briefly refer to three of them.

For one thing, there is the question of accuracy. How accurate are the predictions? Some years ago, we viewed prediction accuracy as fifty-fifty. You could just as well flip a coin. This has changed somewhat. A rough generalisation, which seems to fit the facts, is that today, accuracy has been improved as far as those predicted *not* to recidivate are concerned. A prediction *not* to recidivate is more prone than before to be correct. But for those predicted to recidivate, prediction accuracy is still quite uncertain. A prediction *to* recidivate is not more prone than before to be correct.[27] The latter point is the crux of the matter, a basic flaw as far as effectiveness goes and a most serious finding in terms of legal security.

A second point is the fact that prediction tests are made up, for example, of such factors as unemployment, drug use, social history and the like. Placing people in long-term prison on the basis of predictions using factors like these raises fundamental moral questions – *regardless* of degree of accuracy.

A third point is that reliance on risk and probability is entirely contrary and foreign to sentencing practice and sentencing values in a court room, again regardless of degree of accuracy. The court sentences – and should sentence – people for acts they have committed, not for acts they may commit in the future. There are perhaps exceptions to this, for example as regards mentally unstable persons who have committed very serious crimes, but this is the general rule – and should remain the general rule.[28]

The fact that incapacitation, whether collective or selective, contains basic flaws like these, is a powerful argument against building more prisons. An additional flaw is the fact the crimes of course are committed also behind the walls, while the inmates are under 'incapacitation'. Such crimes at times make big headlines, but are somehow conveniently forgotten when incapacitation is emphasised.

Justice?

In the fourth place, there is the question of justice. The question raises a whole series of complex philosophical and empirical questions. We all want and like justice. But how do we measure it?

There is a vast literature on this question. I have to be brief, and limit myself to the following major point, relevant to criminology and so-called 'neoclassical' criminological thinking:[29] when you try to measure the justice of imprisonment, you convert offensive behaviour into time. Time spent can presumably make up for the offence, and is measured out. You can make a scale, relating specific offences to length of time. Such scales are in frequent use in parts of the United States and elsewhere. The crucial question becomes this: how do you *anchor* the scale? In 1970, a scale like this would be anchored in one place. A two-year sentence for offence X would be considered 'just'. But the winds have changed, the tide has turned. Today we live in a law and order climate. In 2008 a four-year sentence would therefore be considered just for offence X. The point is that the anchor of the scale is not fixed. The anchor changes with time (and also in space).

The fact that the 'justice' of imprisonment, our most painful type of punishment, varies with time, political climate, media opinions, moral panics, and the like, is in itself a powerful argument for at least not building more prisons.

Irreversibility

The first four arguments which I have touched on now, are actually arguments against prisons as such, and not only against building more of them. But they are used here as arguments against further expansion. The next six arguments pertain more specifically to the question of building more prisons; I'll consider them briefly.

The fifth argument is that of the irreversibility of prison-building. Once a prison is built, it will (almost) never be torn down again. You can compare this with a massive case of civil disobedience in the early 1980s in Norway. The focus of the sit-down demonstrations which took place was the construction of a huge dam in a 200 kilometre-long river in northern Norway. The river, the Alta river, is situated in a wild and fantastic canyon, rich in salmon and other wild life, and important to the old indigenous Sami culture. The state's purpose was to produce electricity. We argued *inter alia* that the dam would work at cross purposes to a series of environmental considerations, and that its construction would be irreversible – once built, the dam would never be torn down again. In the end we lost, the dam was built and production of electricity began.[30] The demonstrators were right: the process turned out to be irreversible – despite other sources of energy which are now being developed, the dam with the production of electricity from the river stays on, and will stay on in the foreseeable future.

So it is with prisons. Once built, they remain. A major section of the Oslo prison, Norway's largest prison today, was opened in 1851. It was a 'Philadelphia prison', with small individual cells and extensive isolation of the prisoners, the prison style at the time, and it was the country's major so-called central prison until 1970.[31] At that point, a brand new prison took over the function of being a central prison. The old prison was modernised a bit, and became a part of the Oslo prison. It still is, 157 years after its opening.

A major forced labour institution on the west coast of Norway, mainly taking alcoholic vagrants, was opened in 1915. Forced labour was abolished in 1970, and the forced labour institution closed down. The next day it was reopened as the main regular prison on the west coast. It still is the main prison on the west coast.

A school for boys with 'adjustment problems' was opened in 1898 on the island of Bastøy in the Oslo fjord. After the abolition of forced labour in 1970, it became a 'protection home' for alcoholic vagrants. Many of the old alcoholics who came there had been there as boys with 'adjustment problems'. Subsequently it again became a school, and finally it became a regular prison. As of 2008 – 110 years after its opening as a prison-like kind of school – it is still a prison, one of the solid cornerstones of the Norwegian prison system.

So we could go on. Prisons which are several hundred years old, in the centres of towns and cities, are at times torn down, or converted into something entirely different. Partly, they intervene with business and commerce. Långholmen prison in Stockholm, Sweden, is a case in point. Långholmen started as a work colony for homeless people, prostitutes and beggars in 1724. In 1827 it became a traditional prison. In the 1870s it was rebuilt and became a central cell prison, according to the Philadelphia style of the time. The last prisoner left Långholmen in 1975. In 1989 the story of the prison ended – it was converted into a luxurious hotel, where the guests are invited to spend a pleasant and romantic night. But it had existed as a work colony or prison for 251 years. Several hundred years is a long time; I count such prisons as irreversible constructions.

Insatiability

In the sixth place, a prison system is like an insatiable beast of prey, a predator which is never satisfied. Prisons are almost always filled to the rim, or even overcrowded. Once built, any new prison will be filled to the rim, while old prisons will largely remain. Irreversibility and insatiability interact, fostering each other. Andrew Coyle, Professor of Prison Studies at King's College London and a former prison governor, has this to say about prison-building:

> The reality is that no jurisdiction has ever built its way out of prison overcrowding. The provision of more prison places invariably means that more people are sent to prison. Alexander Paterson, a famous English Prison Commissioner in the 1920s, recognized this fact: 'Wherever prisons are built, Courts will make use of them.'[32]

Inhumanity

In the seventh place, modern prisons will not be more humane than the old ones. At least, this is the case for closed prisons, and is certainly the experience of many prisoners.

In Scandinavia and in the eyes of prisoners, modern closed prisons are often seen as worse than the old ones. The modern closed prisons are made of steel, concrete, special glass and video surveillance. They are degrading, and there is no place to hide, to paraphrase the title of David Bradley's famous book from 1948 on the threat of the atom bomb.[33] In one Norwegian prison, drug control of inmates who have been out on furloughs does not only take place through urine tests and run-of-the-mill searches: you also regularly have to strip, and stand, with your legs apart, on top of a mirror, so that guards get a good view far into your behind. Degrading for prisoners, degrading for guards. For prisoners suspected of smuggling drugs in condoms which they swallow, special toilet facilities exist, where you are forced to sit until you do your thing, the facilities storing your excrement in special plastic bags.

In the old prisons, there are at least places to hide, also for legitimate activity. You have some space of your own. Control is not total. In modern prisons, the goal is to reach total control. The goal is never fully attained; with regard to drugs the controls are actually a failure, so the spiral development of control methods continues. So does inhumanity.

Breaking with values

In the eighth place, irreversible, insatiable and inhumane new prisons break with the basic values of dignity, respect and human rights which all individuals in our society should have access to. More generally, increased reliance on prison, which the construction of new prisons signifies, breaks with the basic values of the welfare state. The values of the welfare state exist at least in the Nordic countries despite the recent neoliberal trend, and, I believe, they exist among the grassroots in Britain and other European states as well.

The building of new prisons is actually an intensification of the war against the poor. Not poverty, but the poor. Above I have pointed out that prisoners are without money, without employment, without education, without housing, often drug addicts, in poor health. Numerous studies in the Nordic countries convincingly show this.[34] The studies (especially Lotte Rustad Thorsen's work), show that the 'further into' the penal system you come, the poorer you are. Those serving unconditional prison sentences – the final stop – are the poorest of all. It is hardly different in other parts of the Western world. The prison populations of the Western world have changed in recent years, including for example more foreigners, but the prisoners' poverty has not changed. The notion that prisons today, as opposed to earlier times, are filled with organised criminals in the possession of great resources, is to a large extent a myth. The building of new prisons, thus intensifying the war against the poor, runs completely counter to basic values of welfare in our society.

Does not help the victim

In the ninth place, the prison does not help the victim. Punishment in terms of time in prison has no natural relationship to the suffering of the victim, and the opening of new prisons does not alleviate the pains of the victim.

There are numerous alternative ways of coming to the aid of the victim. Let me briefly mention three major kinds of what I would call *solidarity-based compensation* to victims. All three are unrelated to time in prison. One is *automatic material compensation*, through an automatic insurance policy organised and financed by the state (very modest fees, as part of the taxation package, would be enough to cover the costs). A second would be *symbolic compensation* in the form of new rituals of sorrow and grief, including resources for processing and going over what has happened as well as new ways of conferring renewed status and dignity. And a third, *social-support networks*, including shelters of various kinds, around victims. Restorative justice is a part of the package.

Overpopulation may be solved in other ways

Remember Andrew Coyle's words, that no jurisdiction has ever built its way out of prison overcrowding. In the tenth place, overpopulation – keeping the prison population 'down to size', making building projects unnecessary – may be restrained in three ways.

Firstly, by advancing the date of release a little. Norwegian legislation has a provision making it possible for prison authorities to advance the date of release by five or ten days. If you shorten all or most sentences by five or ten days, the result is a very large number of empty cells. Advancing the date of release a little was an important method of solving the recent 'queue problem' in Norway – several thousand people waiting in line to serve their sentence. The 'queue' has more or less disappeared.

Secondly, by reintroducing 'release at two-thirds time' as the typical release practice. This was the policy in Norway in the 1970s and 1980s. There were exceptions, but they were relatively few. It worked well, and did not increase the crime rate. Later, rules have been changed, and release at two-thirds time has become less automatic. Remember what I have said about rehabilitation, general prevention and incapacitation. None of these goals will be affected by shorter prison time. If the policy of release at two-thirds time is reintroduced, and introduced elsewhere, the pressure on the prison system will of course decrease. In the 1980s, Sweden used to practise almost automatic release at half time. It was abolished some years ago. It should be reintroduced.

Thirdly, by the shortening of sentences for drug-related crimes. Drug offences internationally carry very stiff sentences, even where minor crimes are concerned. Because so many are involved, even minor shortening of sentences will lower the prison population substantially, making prison-building unnecessary.[35]

These are my ten arguments for not building more prisons. Prisons do not rehabilitate, they do not function as general prevention, they do not work as incapacitation, they do not work in terms of justice, they are irreversible, insatiable, and inhumane, they conflict with basic values, they do not help the victims, and there are other ways of solving overpopulation problems.

As these lines are written in November 2008, there is widespread unrest in several European prison systems. For over two weeks now, nearly six thousand prisoners in Greece – half of the prison population – have been on hunger strike. The protest is directed against the excessive use of remand custody, the unfair administration of parole and temporary release, abusive prison staff, overcrowded and degrading conditions, inadequate medical provisions, etc. During this time, two prisoner deaths and one attempted suicide have been reported, while tens of others have sewn their lips together. At the same time, a hunger strike among prisoners on life sentences is about to start in Italy. There are approximately 1,300 persons serving life sentences in Italian prisons today. Roughly 50 per cent of them are released from prison only after a long period of time. For them, the life sentence means around thirty years. After about fifteen years they may be 'semi-released' (*semilibertá*), which means that they work outside and return to prison at night. After twenty years they may be released on parole (*affidamento al servizio sociale*). The other 50 per cent of the lifers are never released. For them, life imprisonment is really for life. They are thought to be particularly dangerous. They are largely kept under very restrictive and harsh maximum security conditions. Some have been kept in prison for more than forty years.

So there is ferment inside. We should engage ourselves from the outside. As a first demand, I would propose *at least a ten years' moratorium on prison-building*. We should demand this from our national governments and parliaments. We should demand it from regional organisations such as the European Union. We should demand it from the United Nations.

Around such a call and demand, a new international prison movement may develop, inside and outside our prisons. In due course, it might or would turn the tides. It would give us – our governments, our regional institutions, our global organisations – ten years' time for hard thinking around the issue of a more civilised and humane penal policy than we have today.

Notes

1   Editor's note: this text was written in November 2008.
2   Helene Oppen Gundhus, '"For sikkerhets skyld": IKT, yrkeskulturer og kunnskapsarbeid i politiet' ('"To be on the safe side": IT, work cultures and knowledge-based policing'), Ph.D. thesis, Department of Criminology and Sociology of Law, University of Oslo, 2006.
3   Thomas Mathiesen, '*Lex Vigilatoria*: global control without a state?', in Mathieu DeFlem (ed.), *Surveillance and Governance: Crime Control and Beyond* (Bingley, UK: Emerald/JAI Press, 2008), p. 103; information from the House of Lords, European Union Committee 2007. By 2001, thirteen EU states were fully fledged members of Schengen

(UK and Ireland wished to maintain their own border control and stayed partly outside, but participated in police cooperation). Norway and Iceland, non-members of the EU, fully applied the provisions of the Schengen *acquis*, bringing the total number of Schengen member states to fifteen. In 2004 and 2007 a total of twelve Eastern European states were given the status of EU members, and on 21 December 2007 nine of the new EU member states entered the Schengen area, bringing the total number of Schengen members to twenty-four. The figures provided in this essay will no doubt increase as the new members come online. For the text of the *acquis*, see http://eur-lex.europa.eu/ LexUriServ/LexUriServ.do?uri=CELEX:42000A0922(02):EN:HTML (accessed 23 February 2009).

4 Mathiesen, '*Lex Vigilatoria*', p. 104, see note 3. Enormous amounts of information may be found on the website of the British civil liberties organisation Statewatch at www.statewatch.org. For recent developments in the Schengen Information System, see in particular Ben Hayes, 'From the Schengen Information System to SIS II and the Visa Information (VIS): the proposals explained' (2004), at www.statewatch.org/news/ 2005/may/analysis-sisII.pdf (accessed 25 February 2009).

5 For an overview and analysis see e.g. Mathiesen, '*Lex Vigilatoria*', as in note 3.

6 For an account and analysis of the widening of the concept of terrorism in the European Union after 11 September 2001, see e.g. Thomas Mathiesen, 'Expanding the concept of terrorism?', in Phil Scraton (ed.), *Beyond September 11: An Anthology of Dissent* (London: Pluto Press, 2002).

7 See e.g. Thomas Mathiesen, *The Politics of Abolition* (London: Martin Robertson and Oslo: Universitetsforlaget, 1974); Christian G. De Vito, 'Prisoners' movements in Western Europe (1965–2000)', unpublished manuscript, 2004.

8 Permit me to be a bit ethnocentric, and say that the Norwegian Association for Penal Reform, KROM, which was established in 1968, still exists and is active, organising large yearly conferences on penal policy, and having political contact with prisoners inside the walls. See Thomas Mathiesen, 'About KROM – past – present – future' (2000), at www.krom.no/hva_er_krom.php (accessed 25 February 2009).

9 See Stellan Vinthagen, 'Motståndet mot den nya världsordningen' ('The resistance against the new world order'), in Janne Flyhed and Magnus Hörnqvist (eds), *Laglöst land: terroristjakt och rättssäkerhet i Sverige* (*Lawless Land: The War on Terrorism and Legal Security in Sweden*) (Stockholm: Ordfront, 2003).

10 Øyvind Brungot Dahl, Janne Flyghed and Thomas Mathiesen, 'Göteborg 14. til 17. juni 2001: 15 norske beretninger fra EU toppmøtet' ('Gothenburg 14 to 17 June 2001: 15 Norwegian accounts from the EU summit'), obtainable from the Department of Criminology and Sociology of Law, University of Oslo.

11 Thomas Mathiesen, 'The arguments against building more prisons', in Norman Bishop (ed.), *Scandinavian Criminal Policy and Criminology 1980–85* (Oslo: Scandinavian Research Council for Criminology, 1985).

12 For further documentation and detail, I refer to my book *Prison on Trial*, 3rd edn (Winchester: Waterside Press, 2006, originally 1990).

13 For example, in Norway the total failure of our borstal system (*arbeidsskolen*, literally 'the work school'), which constituted long-term incarceration in an open institution with a work and treatment programme for young offenders, is a case in point. Solid empirical

research showed that recidivism was sky-high: Kåre Bødal, *Arbeidsskolen og dens behand-lingsresultater* (*The Borstal and its Treatment Results*) (Oslo: Universitetsforlaget, 1962). The history of the youth prison system, which followed the borstal, tells the same story: Kåre Bødal, *Fra arbeidsskole til ungdomsfengsel: klientel og resultater* (*From Borstal to Youth Prison: Clients and Results*) (Oslo: Universitetsforlaget, 1969).

14 Robert Martinson, 'What works? Questions and answers about prison reform', *Public Interest* 35 (1974).

15 Robert Martinson, 'New findings, new reviews: a note of caution regarding sentencing reform', *Hofstra Law Review* 7 (1979).

16 See e.g. Frank S. Pearson *et al.*, 'Rehabilitative programs in adult corrections: CDATE meta-analyses', paper presented at the Annual Meeting of the American Society of Criminology, San Diego, 22 November 1997; Frank S. Pearson, Douglas Lipton, Charles Cleland and Dorline Yee, 'The effects of behavioral/cognitive-behavioral programs on recidivism', *Crime and Delinquency* 48:3 (2002); Mark W. Lipsey, Nana Landenberger and Gabrielle Chapman, 'Rehabilitation: an assessment of theory and research', in Colin Sumner (ed.), *Blackwell Companion to Criminology* (Oxford: Blackwell Publishers, 2004).

17 A number of other meta-studies show similar results, or show that while various kinds of treatment programmes may have some effect on recidivism in corrections in the outside community, effects are very meagre in the prison setting, which is our concern here. See for example Friedrich Lösel and Martin Schmucker, 'The effectiveness of treat-ment for sexual offenders: a comprehensive meta-analysis', *Journal of Experimental Criminology* 1 (2005). The meta-study includes sixty-nine individual studies. Lösel and Schmucker point out that total effect 'vanishes completely' under some methodological conditions; that 'there was a strong tendency for relatively larger effects in outpatient treatment and smaller effects in institutions'; and that the 'context of treatment is also relevant for outcome. Ambulatory programs [in the community] have larger effects than institutional treatment.' The major problem running through the various meta-studies is *implementation* of treatment programmes (see for example Lipsey in the quote above, p. 106). The prison context is simply not conducive to the treatment programmes in question.

18 Karl F. Schumann, Claus Berlitz and Hans-Werner Guth, *Jugendkriminalität und die Grenzen der Generalprävention* (Berlin: Luchterhand, 1987).

19 Richard A. Wright, *In Defense of Prisons* (London: Greenwood Press, 1994). The econometric studies are generally somewhat more optimistic than others. The debate over the econometric studies focuses *inter alia* on the rationalistic preconditions which the studies and models are based on.

20 Mathiesen, *Prison on Trial*, p. 180, as in note 12.

21 I say 'perhaps' because there are also some doubts regarding the influence of risk of detection on criminal behaviour. Richard Wright, honest defender of prison as he is, also refers to important *panel studies* of the probability of punishment – the risk of detection – which show *no effect* on later crime. However, he refers to methodological problems which may explain these results, and the results do run counter to other research on the risk of detection. The moderate effect of detection risk seems fairly well established.

But here it is important to keep the nature of our modern, anonymous city life in mind. Detection rates are generally very low under such conditions, which also makes the effectiveness of detection risk low in actual practice. More police in the streets would probably improve the rate, but only a massive police force, bringing us more or less to a full scale police state, would be necessary if we were to attain a substantial change in the rate. Most of us do not want a police state.

22 The conclusion that a stiffening of sentences, and increased penalties, has no long-term effect, is also found in other reviews of the research literature. See Andrew von Hirsch, Anthony E. Bottoms, Elizabeth Burney and P.-O. Wikstrom, *Criminal Deterrence and Sentence Severity: An Analysis of Recent Research* (Oxford: Hart, 1999). An extensive review of the research in question is given in my book *Prison on Trial*, pp. 55–84, and pp. 179–83, as in note 12.

23 See Sheldon L. Messinger and Richard A. Berk, 'Review essay: dangerous people' (review of Blumstein *et al.* 1986), *Criminology* 25 (1987).

24 Alfred, Blumstein, J. Cohen, J. Roth and C. A. Visher (eds), *Criminal Careers and 'Career Criminals'* (2 vols, Washington DC: National Academy Press, 1986).

25 *Ibid.*, volume 1, p. 128.

26 For details, see e.g. Thomas Mathiesen, 'Selective incapacitation revisited', *Law and Human Behavior* 22:4 (1998).

27 For more details, see a summary in Mathiesen, *Prison on Trial*, pp. 183–9, as in note 12.

28 The whole development in the police and penal system in the direction of risk orientation – see above – actually runs counter to basic values in our criminal law.

29 For an interesting discussion of neoclassicism, see Katja Franko Aas, *Sentencing in the Age of Information: From Faust to Macintosh* (London: GlassHouse Press, 2005).

30 But in the long run I think we won: altogether, tens of thousands of people participated over several years, placing the environmental issue squarely on the Norwegian political agenda.

31 Editor's note: for more on prison design and the ideas behind it, see S. McConville and L. Fairweather (eds), *Prison Architecture* (Oxford: Architectural Press, 2000); N. Johnston, *Forms of Constraint: A History of Prison Architecture* (Urbana, IL: University of Illinois Press, 2000).

32 Andrew Coyle, 'The limits of the penal system', in *The Principles and Limits of the Penal System: Initiating a Conversation*. Papers from Seminar 1, Commission on English Prisons Today, 2008, p. 12. Coyle also presents convincing data showing that in fact there is no clear relationship between changes in the registered crime rate and changes in the prison rate. The crime rate does not predict the prison rate. Between 1991 and 2001 the crime rate in Canada, Denmark, and England and Wales went *down* by −17 per cent, −9 per cent, and −11 per cent respectively, while the prison rate went up in Canada by +2 per cent, down in Denmark by −9 per cent, and up in England and Wales by +45 per cent (England and Wales have seen an increase in the prison population from 45,000 in 1992 to more than 81,000 in 2007). The crime rate in the Netherlands and Spain increased, during the same period, by +13 per cent and +3 per cent respectively, while the prison rate increased with a whole lot more – notably by +105 per cent and +28 per cent respectively. The prison rate is a consequence of *policy* – political choices

and decisions in view of media coverage, political attitudes, and so on – rather than just automatically following the crime rate.

33 David Bradley, *No Place to Hide* (Boston: Little, Brown, 1948).

34 See e.g. Britta Kyvsgaard, ... *og fængslet tar'r de sidste* (... *And the Prison Takes the Last Ones*) (Copenhagen: Jurist- og økonomiforbundets forlag, 1989); Stig Åhs, Leif Stenberg and Leif Svanström, *Fångarna i välfärdssamhället* (*The Prisoners in the Welfare State*) (Stockholm: Tiden förlag/Folksam, 1991); Anders Nilson and Henrik Tham, *Fångars levnadsförhällanden: resultat från en levnadsnivåundersökning* (*The Life Conditions of Prisoners: Results from a Study of Level of Life Conditions*) (Norrköping: Kriminalvårdsstyrelsen, 1999); Torbjørn Skardhamar, 'Levekår og livssituasjon blant innsatte i norske fengsler' ('Living conditions and life situation among inmates in Norwegian prisons'), Department of Criminology and Sociology of Law, University of Oslo, K-series number 1, 2002; Lotte Rustad Thorsen, *For mye av ingenting ...: straffedes levekår og sosiale bakgrunn* (*Too Much of Nothing ...: The Life Conditions and Social Background of Punished People*) (Oslo: hovedfagsavhandling i kriminologi, Universitetet i Oslo, 2004).

35 (Author's update, July 2009) Interestingly, in February 2009 a federal three-judge panel ruled that the California prison system, the nation's largest with more than 150 thousand prisoners, could reduce its population by shortening sentences, giving inmates good behaviour credits towards early release, reforming parole (which they said would have no adverse effect on public safety), and the like. Without such a plan, the panel said, conditions inside the prisons would continue to deteriorate and inmates would simply die of suicide or lack of proper care (information from *New York Times*, 10 February 2009). In July 2008 California's governor, Arnold Schwarzenegger, proposed to cut the prison population by a sizeable proportion to save the state from total bankruptcy due to the fiscal crisis. Federal courts had already ruled that the state's failure to provide medical and mental healthcare to prisoners had subjected them to cruel and unusual punishment, which is prohibited by the Constitution. This goes to show that the winds may be changing in favour of reducing prison populations rather than building more prisons to solve prison overcrowding.

5a David Downes

Comments on Mathiesen's 'Ten reasons . . . '[1]

Thomas Mathiesen is one of the world's foremost criminologists. Along with his Norwegian compatriot, Nils Christie, he has become over the past forty years a towering figure in thinking about crime and punishment. So when he writes a sustained broadside against penal growth and for a moratorium on prison-building, we should listen very carefully to what he says. The more so because of the very restraint in what he is proposing. For Mathiesen has long been an advocate of far more radical reform – little short of the abolition of the prison system in its entirety. The fact that in this essay he is scaling down his proposals, from the abolition of or substantial reduction in prison populations to simply calling a halt to further expansion, is a sign that things have become markedly worse – in some respects, principally the explosion of mass imprisonment in the USA, far, far worse. The stakes have steadily become, over the past two decades, very high indeed.

Yet it is possible to agree with every single argument Mathiesen makes about the futility and damaging consequences of imprisonment and still disagree with his recommended moratorium. First, in only a minority of societies in the developed world – the USA, Britain, New Zealand and the Netherlands in particular – have prison population rates per 100,000 increased by over 50 per cent over the past twenty years.[2] Several major societies have stable or only moderately increased levels of imprisonment, notably Canada, Germany, France, the Nordic countries and Belgium. Italy fluctuates between a low of 60 per 100,000 and a high of 110. These are not redolent of what has come to be called 'the punitive turn'. Therefore, why should a moratorium be imposed (in principle, as the power to do so is so far lacking) on – in penal reformers' terms – good and bad alike?

Secondly, a ban on fresh prison-building could simply consign ever more prisoners to the miseries of overcrowded cells, unless steps are also taken to rein in the numbers sentenced to custody, and to shorten the length of time served. That raises the vexed question of how to square the circle of growing numbers and a fixed prison estate. The latest idea for a Sentencing Commission to align prison capacity (supply) to prison numbers (demand) was put forward in England by the Carter Review, which notoriously also proposed three new 'Titan' prisons, each containing 2,500 prisoners.[3] That report embodies the kind of contradiction about prison overcrowding which Mathiesen and Andrew Coyle highlight – a Sentencing Commission to calibrate prison capacity to predicted demand, but just let's build three more huge prisons first to solve the immediate problem! However, the problem remains of how to rein in prison numbers without undue encroachment on the independence of the judiciary and the predictable outrage of the tabloid press about contempt for public opinion and the suffering of victims. A related problem is monitoring what is going on institutionally to ensure that quasi-prison alternatives are not being evolved to mask significant numbers.

Thirdly, the moratorium would need to allow for fresh prison-building to replace existing stock that is 'unfit for purpose' for whatever reason. This is not necessarily to fall into the trap of building new prisons to replace clapped-out stock and then finding that the government has decided, after all, to keep the old stock for refurbishment. It could be the case that large and badly designed prisons are replaced by several much smaller prisons far closer to where prisoners' families live – along the lines Lord Woolf recommended in his 1991 report.[4] A moratorium on fresh building should allow for such replacements.

There are other conceivable objections to a moratorium, but these are perhaps the most substantial, barring of course the very processes by which such a moratorium might be accomplished politically. But they do not seem to me to amount to a case against, and I now turn to the strengths of the case for such a move to be broached on an international basis. To that end, there are some points to be made which could state the case more persuasively. These fall into two main headings: first, additional arguments against imprisonment; and secondly, positive outcomes of a moratorium.

There are three main fronts on which I would like to see the case against imprisonment made by Mathiesen bolstered. They are: the 'paradigm shift' caused by the growth of mass imprisonment in the USA; the character of the new politics of crime control; and the counter-intuitive relationship between crime and punishment. On all three fronts, changes over the past few decades greatly strengthen the case for a moratorium on prison-building.

First, the phenomenal growth of prison numbers in the USA since the mid-1970s has shattered the liberal paradigm that the sheer human and financial costs of mass imprisonment effectively rule out such a development in a democracy. Hence, the fact that no other democratic society comes anywhere near the US scale of imprisonment is no great reassurance, for that precedent shows how rapidly it can happen. It was neither planned nor predicted. There were advocates of tougher incapacitation, such as James Q. Wilson, who helped to legitimise what came to happen. But even they gave no sign of appreciating just what the move to harsher penalties would unleash.

The main justification for such a devastating adoption of punitive measures was that they were needed, all else having failed, to halt rising crime rates (on which, see below). What they actually achieved was to demonstrate that there is no natural limit to the growth of prison numbers. At every point along the way, penal reformers have expressed the hope that the scale of imprisonment has peaked – at one million, one-and-a-half million, finally two million – the current figure is 2.35 million and rising. Under these circumstances, a moratorium on prison-building is the most modest policy one could hope for. The fact that it is an unrealistic hope, even in the current reformist climate conjured by the election of President Obama, is no reason to reject it as a stimulus to fresh thinking. If other countries adopt it, it serves as an example to provide a basis for American penal reformers to make the case anew.

The litany of the fallout from mass incarceration in the USA is familiar to every criminologist in the world but barely appreciated by most politicians and citizens even in the USA. In his summation of the adverse effects of mass imprisonment in the USA, Bruce Western documents the extent to which it has damaged the life chances of African-American and Hispanic males in particular.[5] Lifetime earnings have been so depleted that imprisonment alone has significantly increased inequality along lines of colour as well as class. Family break-up has been substantially increased. Political disenfranchisement of felons has robbed several million men of the vote, in some states for life – this factor alone placed George W. Bush in the White House in 2000. Western concludes by assessing the impact as going far to reversing all that was won by the Civil Rights Movement of the 1960s.

Mass imprisonment in the USA has become a factor in political economy in its own right. Its impact on the unemployment rate, by excluding some two million prisoners of working age and by including as employed those working as 'guard labour', has increasingly made the USA's economic performance look far better than it deserves for some two decades.[6] Opponents of European social democracy have traded on this gap. The vast and growing expenditures on custody have depleted welfare budgets for the public services of health and education. Prison staff unions are a growing force in state and national politics. The political economy of the USA is now locked into a vast prison-industrial complex which will be hugely resistant to any halt, let alone reduction in size and resources.

Secondly, the new politics of crime control has fostered this drift towards mass imprisonment. The key to this development is the electoral advantage gained by parties which mount claims to be 'tough on crime' (with or without the rider – 'tough on the causes of crime'). However, this adoption of endless contestation between rival parties for who can be 'toughest' on crime seems to have taken root only in the neoliberal political economies of the USA, Britain and New Zealand. Most social democratic countries, with the partial exception of the Netherlands, have mounted a vigorous resistance to its seductions. A key argument for a moratorium on prison-building is the removal of the central electoral card of commitments to building yet more prisons. In the British 2005 election, the Conservatives pledged to build twenty thousand more prison places. The Labour Government have since pledged to build just short of that number. This ratcheting up of prison places is in perpetual play as a factor in what Jonathan Simon has termed 'governing through crime' – the embedded assumption that being in any conceivable way 'soft on crime' is tantamount to disqualification for office.[7]

Again, there is a formidable fallout from such politics, less destructive than in the USA but still substantial and increasingly oppressive. Such penal populism also generates a constant erosion of civil liberties, with already unjustifiable levels of surveillance, identity controls and net-widening being remorselessly extended. Thus, neoliberal political economy, the turbo-capitalist model that generated the current recession, is also strongly associated with high levels of imprisonment, eroding civil liberties, and the lowest ages of criminal responsibility. The over-control of lower-class deviance, as in Anti-Social Behaviour Orders, brought in by New Labour in 1998, is accompanied by the under-regulation of corporate finance. It almost goes without saying that a moratorium on prison-building will be most resisted where it is most needed – in 'first-past-the-post' political economies where 'governing through crime' has become embedded as a way of life politically and culturally. But that is not an argument for dropping the whole idea.

Thirdly, Thomas Mathiesen correctly argues that a key part of the case for imprisonment rests on the fallacy that crime rates fall as a deterrent consequence of tougher custodial sentencing. In my view, criminologists need to work far harder on this question if they are to convince people in general that the dynamics of crime and punishment are largely independent of each other.[8] That is – after all – massively counter-intuitive. However, on one key issue, capital punishment, criminologists helped to win a notable victory – so much so that the abolition of capital punishment is now a prerequisite for membership of the European Union. How was this achieved? Partly at least because generations of criminologists produced exhaustive data on the *lack of* relationship between capital punishment and homicide.[9] The relationships between crimes and punishments are yet more complex and, in certain conditions, it may be the case that sharply rising crime does indeed produce tougher punishments. However, comparatively speaking, the evidence of trends is cumulatively against either more crime leading necessarily to more punishment or more punishment leading to less crime (see especially Lappi-Seppälä 2008).[10] Perhaps the most striking contrast of all is the compelling symmetry between fluctuations in the homicide rates in the USA and Canada. Over the past forty years, they have risen and fallen more or less simultaneously, despite the fact that the Canadian prison population rate has remained much the same, while the

American has expanded five or even six-fold. And the rate of homicide in Canada has remained one-third lower than that of the USA throughout the entire period. Bruce Western has estimated that fully 90 per cent of the fall in crime rates in the USA over the past fifteen years would have occurred without mass imprisonment. If we are to dislodge the master-narrative of crime and punishment – that 'prison works' – we must do more to publicise the mismatch between rhetoric and reality on this front.

Not only that, but a counter-narrative is needed, which brings me to the second set of points – how a moratorium might lead to more positive thinking about punishment and control. Penal reformers have long argued that the alternative to prison is not doing nothing but doing something else of a more constructive and less damaging nature. The list is long and varied, from the standard non-custodial penalties of the fine, probation and community service, to the more recently developed alternatives grouped around the concept of 'restorative justice' originally and tirelessly propounded by John Braithwaite since his 1989 book *Crime, Shame and Reintegration*.[11] The core idea of that book is that *reintegrative* forms of inducing or fostering shame in offenders, for the pains they have inflicted on victims by their misdeeds, are most effectively practiced in relatively non-punitive societies. By contrast, *disintegrative* forms of shaming, which emphasise the need to inflict pain on the offender, most commonly by the over-use of imprisonment, are counter-productive. In the latter, the offender comes to see himself or herself as the real victim, and utilises endless mind games by way of denial and neutralisation of guilt to ward off any insight into their own offending behaviour. Only by a process of mediation, in which offenders and victims meet to thrash out the abuse of power implicit in the offence, and evolve appropriate forms of reparation, can this construction of the offender as victim be confronted and at least partially resolved.

There are certain self-limiting features to restorative justice which have to be acknowledged. First, the processes of face-to-face mediation work far better with personal victims than with institutional victims. There is rather more potential for expressing and experiencing regret for one's actions to a family shaken by burglary or to a small shopkeeper struggling to cope with endless thefts than to the manager of a chain of superstores. Secondly, not all victims wish to take part in dialogue with offenders, however well orchestrated by trained mediators. So one cannot expect restorative justice to cover the waterfront of all crimes, offenders and victims to equal effect. What one *can* expect is for restorative principles of proven worth to be put to work as far as possible in other forms of sentencing, even in prisons themselves.

There are some common objections to restorative justice which are invalid, but which are trotted out as if they automatically end all argument. One is that there is no evidence for such forms of justice as effective. A growing volume of research data is being marshalled to show that these processes work as well as and, in some ways better than, standard forms of justice. Larry Sherman and Heather Strang have shown that restorative approaches work especially well for victims, certainly by comparison with court procedures, which in general marginalise victims to the minimum presence required for cross-examination.[12] In addition, it is often contended that restorative principles work only with the most trivial offences, such as juvenile shoplifting or theft from cars. Older and more experienced and/or violent offenders would not be touched by such measures. Again, Sherman and Strang document growing evidence against this view. Most strikingly, Declan Roche has studied pioneering forms of restorative justice in relation to patterns of serious violence in Cali, Columbia.[13] Columbia is one of the most violence-torn nations on earth. If restorative justice can work there, it can arguably work anywhere. In this set of instances, brutal and corrupt policing made no headway whatsoever against predatory urban gangs. What worked far better was a series of community engagements, led largely by local women, with those most involved in both domestic and street violence.

Roche is careful to spell out certain caveats against the view that restorative justice is a simple recipe for more effective crime control. The Cali project was inspired by a charismatic leader whose

> determination and leadership carries the programme, especially at key moments when obstacles appear and other people are not as committed. If this is true, where does this leave the communities that do not have the benefit of an Hermana Alba Stella to organize and inspire? This is a real problem, but the experience of the women of Aguablanca also provides a valuable reminder that even the most marginalized members of the most marginalized communities have the capacity to change their own lives and to help others change theirs.[14]

Secondly, the programme did not displace but complemented official agencies which had won the trust of local people. While the police are distrusted, the *consejeras*, some of whom are trained as Justices of the Peace, work with two local prosecutors whom they do trust. Thirdly, while informal dispute resolution and reparation remain the core of the criminal justice aspect of their work, their more extensive programme shows how 'restorative justice can take a number of forms. It is as much about teaching young people skills that will allow them to live as law-abiding members of the community, as it is about mediation after a conflict. Restorative justice, in the hands of the consejeras, is not just an approach to conflict resolution, but a framework for advancing social justice.'[15]

These considerations give one confidence that restorative justice does indeed have the potential to act as a counterweight and a counter-narrative to the 'prison works' narrative that has become a mantra in the neoliberal world. It does seem to be the case that where governments have backed such a counter-strategy, the appeal of 'prison works' can be resisted. To revert to the Canadian example, it was in Canada that cognitive behaviour therapies, the foundation for the 'risk-needs-responsivity' model, were developed most successfully over the past few decades. That pioneering work has since been the basis for rehabilitative programmes both in the community and within prisons around the world that have much in common with restorative principles. It does not do much to blunt penal expansionism where that trend has become embedded. But it has arguably done much to restrain it in societies which have not yet subscribed to the new politics of crime control. It has generated fresh thinking as the basis for what Tony Ward and Shadd Maruna term the 'good lives model of rehabilitation', where the key question is not the somewhat mechanistic 'what works?' but 'what helps people go straight?'[16] In *Rehabilitation*, Ward and Maruna state that those who have been 'the most influential and important voice of support for evidence-based correctional policy (as opposed to penal populism or punitive retributivism) for the past thirty years' are 'most often referred to as "the Canadians" (even though their numbers include representations from nearly every continent) ... They have even been credited with "saving" rehabilitation from a premature death ... What they have achieved has required intellectual courage, painstaking precision, stamina, creativity, rigor and perseverance.'[17]

The same qualities will be needed if a compelling case for a moratorium on prison-building is to be made. Thomas Mathiesen has spelt out the basic arguments. They now need to be built on to lasting effect.

Notes

1 Editor's note: this text was written in February 2009.
2 For several years one needed to differentiate England and Wales from Scotland in terms of penal expansion, but after a period of stability, the numbers in Scottish jails have been climbing rapidly too.
3 'Securing the future: proposals for the efficient and sustainable use of custody in England and Wales', the report of Lord Carter's Review of Prisons (2007), available at www.justice.gov.uk/docs/securing-the-future.pdf (accessed 28 February 2009). (Author's update): In April 2009 the Minister of Justice Jack Straw revised the policy, rejecting the proposed three new 'Titan' prisons that would hold 2,500 prisoners each, in favour of five new prisons each holding 1,500 prisoners. The expansionist trend remains unchanged. (See http://news.ssc.co.uk/1/hi/uk/802/222.stm, accessed 16 July 2009.)
4 'The Woolf Report: a summary of the main findings and recommendations of the inquiry into prison disturbances' (London: Prison Reform Trust, 1991).
5 Bruce Western, *Punishment and Inequality in America* (New York: Russell Sage, 2006).
6 Nicola Lacey, *The Prisoners' Dilemma: Political Economy and Punishment in Contemporary Democracies* (Cambridge: Cambridge University Press, 2008), pp. 134–6.
7 Jonathan Simon, *Governing through Crime* (Oxford: Oxford University Press, 2007).

8 Which is not to say that the question has been ignored. Far from it: see, for example, the authoritative analysis by Andrew von Hirsch, Anthony Bottoms, Elizabeth Burney and P.-O. Wikstrom, *Criminal Deterrence and Sentence Severity* (Oxford: Hart, 1999). To the convinced retributivist, of course, the entire 'what works?' question is irrelevant. 'An eye for an eye' is to be preferred even if it makes for more rather than less crime.

9 'Some protagonists of abolition give priority to their fundamental belief that the death penalty is a violation of the human right to life ... But it has to be recognized that in many societies this view is still not self-evident and whether it is embraced or not will in part be determined by the extent to which it can be shown that the death penalty does or does not serve the penal purposes claimed for it.' Roger Hood, *The Death Penalty: A World-Wide Perspective* (Oxford: Clarendon Press, 1996), pp. 5–6.

10 Tapio Lappi-Seppälä, 'Trust, welfare, and political culture: explaining differences in national penal policies', in Michael Tonry (ed.) *Crime and Justice, Volume 37* (Chicago: Chicago University Press, 2008).

11 John Braithwaite, *Crime, Shame and Reintegration* (Cambridge: Cambridge University Press, 1989).

12 Larry Sherman and Heather Strang, *Restorative Justice: The Evidence* (London: Smith Institute, 2007).

13 Declan Roche, 'Governance and restorative justice in Cali, Columbia', in Tim Newburn and Paul Rock (eds) *The Politics of Crime Control* (Oxford: Clarendon Press, 2006).

14 Roche, *ibid.*, p. 282.

15 *Ibid.*, p. 291.

16 Tony Ward and Shadd Maruna, *Rehabilitation: Beyond the Risk Paradigm* (London: Routledge, 2006), p. 107.

17 *Ibid.*, p. x.

6 Jack Mapanje

Creative incarceration and strategies for surviving freedom

The delights of moving house

For what it's worth, I want to tell you the story of how my family and I have been surviving our freedom since we arrived in the UK. I was adopted as a prisoner of conscience by Amnesty International, Pen International, Africa Watch, Human Rights Watch, and many other associations and organisations of writers, linguists, scholars and human rights activists throughout the world – the list is limitless – and it is impossible to pay proper and adequate tribute to them all, except perhaps in the form of this essay, which I also consider a kind of progress report on how this prisoner of conscience has fared after being freed from Mikuyu prison in Malawi many years ago.

My family and I will have been living in the UK for sixteen years this August 2007. Oxford was the first city that welcomed us. We stayed initially with Megan Vaughan and her daughter Anna; we then moved permanently to the city of York, where we stayed with Landeg White and his family before we found accommodation of our own. Both families had been instrumental in my release from prison. Landeg was the de facto UK chairperson for the campaign for my liberation – individuals and groups of campaigners who wanted to know what was happening to me in prison and my family in Malawi consulted him. And Megan was one of the many couriers of news from the UK to my family throughout the three and a half years of my imprisonment.

Two colleagues teaching in the University of Malawi at the time, Father Pat O'Malley and David Kerr, were the crucial contacts in Malawi, without whom Landeg would have got no substantive news to pass on to the world about what was happening. Besides, David had persuaded Richard Carver, who lived in Oxford, worked for Africa Watch and Amnesty International, and had links with radio stations and newspapers, to join Landeg and others in reporting the development of the campaign for my liberation to the wider world. But Landeg was the main star who read from my poems at various venues and publicised my case globally to radio stations, newspapers, human rights groups, compatriots and friends. The famous trio of Landeg, David and Father Pat contacted and appealed to human rights organisations and to British members of the European Parliament (MEPs), the House of Lords and the House of Commons; even the then young black London MP Diane Abbott wrote a letter to President Hastings Banda to demand my release. At the instigation of John La Rose the London community of African Caribbean writers, journalists and ordinary citizens joined the campaign for my release. The late Scottish politicians John Smith and Donald Dewar, MEPs, academics and ordinary freedom lovers in Scotland, and senators in the US and Canada were involved in the campaign for my liberation too; at one point Landeg White even approached the principal of Eton College to see if he could exert influence in my favour on the Malawian dictator – the trio left no stone unturned. And all this not to mention the campaigns that were being mounted in Africa as far apart as Nigeria, Botswana, Zaire, Zimbabwe, Tanzania and Soweto Township in South Africa.

The warmth of welcome and reunion with friends and acquaintances, which we experienced in Oxford and York, helped to heal the scars of incarceration and to soften the pain of exile. There was a social whirl of parties and readings organised by Megan, Landeg and their friends; bottles of champagne were opened for the first time since my freedom. A particular joy was to hear first hand, from Landeg, Megan and many others, how delicate the process of campaigning for my freedom and of carrying news and gifts to my family had been. Yet throughout this early period in the UK, I remained dazed, unbelieving, not certain that I had actually been freed.

It was not until Gillian Tindall, Lady Antonia Fraser, Alastair Niven and others organised a service of thanksgiving for us in London at St Bride's Church, Fleet Street, that we truly felt free. The host of Pen International's Writers in Prison Committee, Amnesty International and others were delighted that their campaign for my release had succeeded. We were humbled to discover that our story was a source of joy to people in many African, European and North American cities. The senators, MEPs, MPs, Lords and other politicians; the writers, linguists, academics, journalists, broadcasters, doctors, churchmen and churchwomen, students, compatriots, friends and strangers – all of those who had fought for my freedom – were pleased that we had arrived safely in the UK. I visited branches of human rights and academic organisations that had adopted me as their prisoner of conscience in the Netherlands, Germany, Austria, Norway, Sweden, Canada, the US, and throughout the UK as well as in African countries.

But eventually the visits and parties had to come to an end. We had to face the stark reality that we were in a foreign land, without a permanent source of income – and there were five of us who needed to develop strategies for surviving freedom in our new home. I had been invited as a visiting scholar at the Centre for

Southern African Studies of the University of York, where Landeg White was director, but I was financially supported, initially for two years, by the Society for the Protection of Science and Learning (now called the Council for Assisting Refugee Academics – CARA) in London. The first shock was the length of the queue for a council house or flat in York. While Landeg White was on leave in Portugal, Megan Vaughan came from Oxford to help us find a privately rented house at 79 Seventh Avenue, Tang Hall, where we attracted a lot of local attention.

Apparently we were the first foreigners of African descent that the neighbours ever encountered. We did not know that York had very few 'people of colour' and that this would become an issue to contend with. We were not prepared for the kind of freedom where we became daily objects of curiosity. But having been liberated from the jaws of African crocodiles we made a joke of the forms of harassment that we suffered:

> **The Delights of Moving House, Tang Hall, York**[1]
> When we first arrived in Tang Hall
> The children welcomed us by stealing
> Glances at us, sniggering over the hedge,
> Milling about the front door hedge after school,
> Spitting loudly, monkey faking without ambiguity
> Until some started throwing eggs at our windows,
> Sometimes writing 'Fuck Off' on the windscreen
> Of the car we had bought near the scrap-yard.
> Judy's laughter fired,
> 'How dare crowds of Tang Hall kids do this to chaps
> Just rescued from the jaws of African crocodiles?'
> Lunda joked,
> 'I wish they gave us the eggs they waste on our walls!'
> Lika merely sulked as he mended his bicycle;
> Mercy frenetically mopped the kitched floor
> Shouting, 'Hold on, children, what lies here?'
> And I thumped my chest recalling my Latin
> 'Mea culpa, mea culpa, mea maxima culpa!'
> I've sinned, I've sinned, I've sinned most grievously.

The Chattering Wagtails of Mikuyu Prison

Today, more than fifteen years on, we often wonder how we survived on the financial assistance we received from the Society, for we barely managed to pay the house rent and fuel bills, or for the children's school uniforms, food and transport. But for the first time in the safety of our foreign environment, we had time to reflect on how God had saved our lives, and how we were going to thank the many individuals and organisations that had fought for our freedom. In Mikuyu prison we had lots of time to develop strategies for what I called creative incarceration: we wrote notes on toilet paper and wrappers of Lifebuoy and Sunlight soap, and smuggled them out to family and friends, telling them about our health; we begged visiting relatives and friends for food and medicines, though often we had these smuggled into prison too. Banda and his inner circle were never ashamed of starving to death the presumed enemies they imprisoned for nothing. We had to develop whatever strategies for survival we could invent. But as no political prisoner was tried or charged and, therefore, no-one knew when we would be released, if we would be released at all, we had not developed strategies for confronting the relative freedom we were to enjoy in the UK.

And when I sought employment, I was not prepared for the racism that glared at me even at the job interviews where I knew I had done well but was told I should try elsewhere. My frustrations were enormous. When human rights organisations fight for the liberation of the prisoners of conscience they have adopted and the prisoners are eventually freed, everyone rejoices, but when the prisoners are subsequently left alone in the wider world to fend for themselves, life becomes another hard pill to swallow. That's a fact. I recharged other creative energies and began working on my second book of poems, which had been interrupted by my imprisonment. After another year and a rigorous interview for the post of Writer in Residence at Durham prison (irony of endless ironies!) three arts boards in England – Northern Arts, Yorkshire and Humberside Arts and North Western Arts – jointly put together a rescue plan, and invited me to become their first Greater North International Writer in Residence; notwithstanding the mouthful title by which I was called, I was delighted to accept the offer.

It was a grey and cold English winter, and for ten months I was the proud passenger of TransPennine Express Railways, shivering from County Durham all the way to Liverpool – I recommend everything except the pallid coffee and stale sandwiches that became my daily bread! I read from my verse and ran creative writing workshops in Frankland prison, Durham prison, Wakefield prison and Garth prison. I discussed African literature and culture with willing reading groups in public libraries, community and city centres, and schools and colleges from Durham to Liverpool and the towns and villages in between. Yet I knew all along that what I needed was a job and a regular salary. And quickly. I was aware that my imprisonment had not provided me with the opportunity to publish papers in linguistics that would help me find a suitable job.

In Malawi, after my doctorate degree in linguistics from University College London (UCL), I had been working on two unpublished papers in linguistics. The first was a phrase structural fragment on 'Agreement phenomenon in Bantu languages' and the second I called 'The ghost of temporal distance' for Bantu language speakers. I had presented the first in Paris at a UNESCO conference on African and Caribbean linguistics and the second at a Botswana University conference of African academics.

Sadly the Special Branch had trampled on both papers when they violently searched and ransacked my house on my arrest and when I returned from prison after four academic years, I found that I had no library to speak of; the cockroaches and other insects had chewed my books. I had co-founded LASU, the Linguistics Association for SADC (Southern African Development Community) Universities, which included nine universities of Africa south of the Sahara, minus apartheid South African universities, and was elected chairperson. Through LASU I had hoped to publish an anthology of essays in linguistics to be used as a text in the colleges and universities of the region. My imprisonment gave me no opportunity to complete the project or to blossom as a linguist. At any rate when I arrived in the UK the linguistics departments in Yorkshire universities did not know that they had an African linguist among them whose experience they could make the most of. My theoretical linguistics would have gone somewhat rusty anyway, so I sought other ways of exploiting my pragmatics.

I remembered that I once considered myself an expert in 'African oral literature' – what we call African orature. In the 1980s I had done research on the subject and, with Landeg White, had compiled and edited *Oral Poetry from Africa: An Anthology*, which was published in 1983 by Longmans UK – for several years the anthology had been a textbook for schools, colleges and universities in parts of Africa. I recalled particularly two research projects that I was engaged in before my imprisonment: the interpretation of African riddles and how it impacted on the reading of written texts, and the interpretation of aspect and tense systems for Bantu language speakers – I was hoping to exploit what is called relevance theory for both projects. I decided to revive my research on both topics. And at the instigation of Professor Terry Ranger, St Anthony's and Exeter Colleges, Oxford, shared me, as it were, for six months, when I was able to use the Bodleian and other rich facilities of Oxford libraries for my research in riddles. The project was later facilitated by personal grants that I was awarded from the Leverhulme Trust and the Wingate Foundation. And a preliminary exploratory article on the project called 'Riddling the politics of Afrocentric literary theory', which suggested that pragmatics (relevance theory) had the potential for the interpretation of literature, was published in Portugal in volume two of *Op. Cit.: A Journal of Anglo-American Studies*.

In 1993 Heinemann International, Oxford, published my second book of poems in their African Writers Series – I called it *The Chattering Wagtails of Mikuyu Prison*. I began to feel that my exile was bearing fruit, though we were painfully aware that neither poetry nor academic research offered us sufficient financial rewards for surviving freedom. We had to look to other projects for that, and often I shamelessly returned to the Society for the Protection of Science and Learning for further financial assistance. I continued to apply for jobs without much success. My wife then decided to retrain as a staff nurse. Within six months she completed her programme at York District hospital. She was then told to work for another six months without pay, after which she was employed permanently as a staff nurse at the hospital. With the grace of God the family finally had an effective breadwinner.

Looking for a subject to teach

I did not stop applying for jobs. And when the School of English at the University of Leeds advertised for a personal professorial chair, I jumped at the idea and tried my luck, expecting to revive my research on the interpretation of literature using linguistic theory. I was happily shortlisted for interview, which was so rigorous that I thought, at long last, I had found what I had been looking for and could settle down at Leeds. It was not to be. Instead the School offered me a flattering huge title: Visiting Professorial Fellow, and an office from where I could reflect on my incarceration and freedom. I was grateful for both and soon began looking for ways of making myself useful as a Visiting Professorial Fellow. When a colleague cynically wondered what I could teach British students after four academic years in an African prison, I laughed at the apparent joke, albeit a painful and cruel one. In prison I had learnt the art of laughing at myself rather than moaning about people. I took the cue seriously and began to think about what I could actually teach in British schools, colleges and universities apart from linguistics. My colleague's question rankled on my mind. Indeed what could I teach anybody after four academic years of crushing mosquitoes and scorpions at night and admiring the antics of rats and cockroaches running around the rafters of my prison cells?

Another problem reared its ugly head. While I was in prison the Gulf War had been and gone, the Berlin Wall had crumbled and with it the Cold War and Iron Curtain, Nelson Mandela had been released in South Africa and the notorious system of apartheid officially abolished. I had a lot to catch up on. And more importantly, after four academic years of not being allowed a pen, paper, newspapers or radio, and with only three Bibles to be shared among ninety political and condemned prisoners for our library – after gazing at filthy prison walls for so long – I had almost forgotten how to read. I had not imagined that this would be a problem, but I must confess that I found it difficult to complete reading even my favourite novel, *Pride and Prejudice*, which in better times I read once a year. Even flicking through the pages of the *Guardian* or the *Times Literary Supplement*, which had been my favourite habit when I was a student in London, seemed cumbersome; I felt like I wanted to continue staring at blank walls.

Nonetheless I forced myself to read and re-read seriously what was once known as 'Third World literature'. On critically examining the articles that purported to explain this literature, however, I found myself suddenly wanting. A component of the Third World literature that I had known as Commonwealth literature, which had been effectively created in the School of English at Leeds University, was now being called postcolonial literature. And literary critics, historians, sociologists, anthropologists and other academics engaged in cultural studies happily assumed the relevance of postcolonial theory in discussions of their respective disciplines. I soon noticed that the theory had become so powerful that every discipline engaged in cultural studies seemed to want to exploit it. I felt excluded. Scared. Especially when I discovered that the postcolonial theoretic interpretation of literature did not seem to adequately illuminate the subject matter of the texts as I thought it might. In certain cases I had a sneaking feeling that the texts were being relegated to the background in favour of theory and theorists – all of which did not augur well for an observer just back from incarceration. I spent sleepless nights reading and re-reading the arguments I had missed while I was put away, until it dawned on me that the postcolonial theory I was hoping would illuminate particularly more recent 'Third World writings' seemed to have transformed itself into a monster so powerful that it probably needed some constraining.

When we read linguistics at UCL we enjoyed the jokes about linguistic theories that seemed to claim too much explanatory power: the best way of handling all-pervasive, all-powerful theories was to constrain them, we thought. I could not think how best to constrain postcolonial theory for my purposes. So I let it pass and mushroom without my meddling with it, conceding in the end that perhaps I didn't understand it after all. I assured myself that the theory would probably became too powerful and die a natural death; or it would be replaced by another with more explanatory adequacy – I recalled theories in linguistics that had suffered a similar fate.

Then I began to re-read African prison poetry, diaries and memoirs, starting with those by Dennis Brutus, Wole Soyinka, Ngugi wa Thiong'o, Breyten Breytenbach, Hugh Lewin, Albie Sachs and others. I wanted to rediscover how other imprisoned writers had survived their incarceration and liberation, wondering all the while whether I could make this an exciting subject of study for students and hoping I might learn one or two tricks from the predecessors I revered in the hope that I would write my own prison memoir one day. After adding the writings on the Holocaust, the Russian gulag and Latin American exiles to my repertoire of African texts, I boldly told my colleagues at Leeds that I was ready to offer students three optional literature modules: Creative Writing, African-Caribbean Orature and what I called Literatures of Incarceration – these were areas where I knew I could use my linguistics with ease.

Most colleagues seemed fine with the first two modules, but not so sure about what I called Literatures of Incarceration. Did I seriously expect British students to sign up for that, one sceptic asked. I had done my homework, I stubbornly protested in defence. And indeed to our shock eighty students signed up for the module. But because I was only a Visiting Professorial Fellow, that is, without a permanent slot on the staff, the student numbers had to come down to thirty-three. I did not understand why. The students signed up nonetheless. We began. And of the three new modules Literatures of Incarceration became the most engaging. It was new and fresh, and students did not have to be versed in critical works by Michel Foucault, Mikhail Bakhtin or Hommi Bhabha to analyse the texts – they rather cherished the idea of becoming critics of a subject that did not appear to have established theorists to contend with. And as one student claimed after receiving her degree, because of the experience she had gained by studying the module, she was able to take employment with one of the human rights organisations in London – I felt a sense of satisfaction and for once thought that my debt to human rights organisations might have been repaid.

Then Martin Mooij at Rotterdam Poetry International in the Netherlands offered me the writer's residency based at the African Studies Centre of the University of Leiden. It was to be paid for by the Ludo Pieters Guest Writer Fund, which would buy me a laptop, a cassette recorder and offer me students to quiz me about how I survived my incarceration in Mikuyu prison. This was the origin of the research in what would eventually become my prison memoir. I returned to Leeds with several tapes of recordings, which I have been using to draft the prison memoir now in progress.

However, after three academic years at Leeds, whoever was paying for my visiting professorial fellowship stopped. I was disappointed and wondered why. Had I outlasted my visit? Did someone fear that I might become a permanent feature in the school? Or was it John Major's cuts in university budgets that did it, as someone suggested? I did not know. But suddenly I had an office without employment. I started applying for jobs again. For periods of three and six months respectively I was writer in residence in the Department of English and Comparative Literature at Warwick University and in the Department of Literature in the Open University at Milton Keynes. These led to the publication of my third book of poems, *Skipping Without Ropes*, by Bloodaxe Books, in 1998. Immediately after this I accepted the writer's residency at University College Cork in the Republic of Ireland, where I started in earnest sketching and drafting my prison memoir. After University College Cork, the Royal Literary Fund Fellowship Scheme took me on, and for three years I was their fellow based at Trinity and All Saints University College, Leeds.

Meanwhile Heinemann International, Oxford, had accepted my proposal that I compile and edit an anthology of African prison writings based on a fragment of the Literatures of Incarceration module that I had taught in the School of English at Leeds – we called the anthology *Gathering Seaweed: African Prison Writing*. It was published in 2002 in their Heinemann African Writers Series. In part it was this anthology that contributed to my getting the Fonlon-Nichols Award from the African Literature Association in the US that year, though I was told I was honoured for my contribution to poetry and human rights. When the anthology appeared I had already moved to Dove Cottage, where Robert Woof, Director of the

Wordsworth Trust, had offered me the writer's residency. It was at Grasmere where I completed the first draft of my prison memoir as I compiled my poetry collection, to be called *The Last of the Sweet Bananas: New and Selected Poems*, which was published in 2004 by Bloodaxe Books in association with the Wordsworth Trust. After three fruitful years at Dove Cottage, I applied for a job in the School of English at the University of Newcastle, where I teach creative writing, with Literatures of Incarceration and Memoir Writing as core modules.

So from the creative incarceration of Mikuyu prison I have ended up inventing principally Literatures of Incarceration, which is a fully-fledged university literature module that has become my survival kit as a writer and an academic in the UK. And having taught this module for many years now I have the nerve to recommend without reservation that all universities that teach cultural studies or consider literature, human rights and freedom worth serious academic attention must include some variant of Literatures of Incarceration on their programme: students love the subject; it is relevant to issues that matter to modern society; and it opens up employment opportunities for students more directly than other literature programmes.

Meanwhile I have not stopped reading from my poetry, talking about African literatures and culture or running creative writing workshops in colleges, community centres, libraries, prisons and schools. These days I take pride in having read from my work and run creative writing workshops as far away as the Shetland and Orkney Islands in Scotland and Cardiff and Swansea in Wales, and throughout England. In each of these places I have been paying tribute to the noble work of the friends and strangers who fought for my freedom; to human rights organisations such as Amnesty International, Pen International, Africa Watch, Human Rights Watch and Article 19; and to academic organisations like the Linguistics Association of Great Britain, the Linguistics and Literature Associations for SADC Universities in Africa, the Association of Nigerian Authors, the Association of African Literature in the US, and many others, shamelessly declaring how they saved my life.

'This prison where I live'

The founder of Amnesty International, Peter Benenson, once made the following observation, which was critical in the formation of his organisation. 'Open your newspaper – any day of the week – and you will find a report from somewhere in the world of someone being imprisoned, tortured or executed because his opinions or religion are unacceptable.'[2] When Benenson made these remarks, he was obviously bothered by the politics of his time and reacting to the timeless problems of incarceration of presumed rebels in societies around the globe.

Merely suspected political dissidents in the USSR were still being sent to appalling gulags and other forms of labour camps in Siberia; the Jews had not recovered from the horrific interrogations, torture and deaths in the notorious gas chambers they encountered under Hitler during the Holocaust. There were atrocious interrogations, torture and disappearances of presumed political opponents in Ceausescu's Romania, in Idi Amin's Uganda, Ian Smith's Rhodesia, Hastings Banda's Malawi, General Augusto Pinochet's Chile and other Latin American countries. Other horrors appeared in apartheid South Africa. And this is to name only a few despotic regimes that might have given birth to an organisation like Amnesty International for Benenson.

Today we live in societies which are becoming increasingly 'prisonised', to borrow a term from Angela Davis, where citizens are categorised on the basis of colour, race, religion and beliefs, where governments spend huge sums of money buying arms to protect its rulers, where clinics or hospital wards are closing down, and more prisons or prison-like structures against refugees and asylums seekers are being constructed instead.[3] For the US the situation has become more desperate and poignant since 9/11, as exemplified by the reports compiled in the publication *Challenging U.S. Human Rights Violations Since 9/11*.[4] The book makes depressing reading.

Take one. 'During Saddam Hussein's regime, Abu Ghraib, situated twenty miles away from Baghdad, served as a prison for up to 50,000 women and men simultaneously, who were subjected to daily tortures and executions ... In April 2003, following the fall of Hussein, the US military took over Abu Ghraib, cleaned and repaired it, and converted it into a US military prison. The prisoners [that the US military brought to Abu Ghraib] were overwhelmingly civilians randomly gathered during military sweeps and at checkpoints, including common criminals, individuals thought to have committed "crimes against the coalition", and suspected insurgents.'[5] The event that the book describes starkly demonstrates how US troops have tortured Iraqis since they invaded their country.

Take two. 'On May 16, 2003, US forces who were chasing looters [in Iraq] arrested ... thirty-one-year-old twin brothers ... [who] were not allowed to wash or have sufficient drinking water. They were not interrogated. After twenty days of detention, [the brothers] were told that they would be released but instead were taken to Abu Ghraib prison ... On June 12, 2003, all detainees [at Abu Ghraib] demonstrated against their detention conditions ... Amnesty International delegates saw numerous ex-detainees with wrists still scarred by the cuffs a month later.'[6]

The book offers more heart-rending revelations, which challenge the nature of the 'civilised' world of the twenty-first century. In recent times television screens around the world have been inundated with similar horrific pictures and images of innocent Iraqis tortured by US and British soldiers. But I am not qualified to review *Challenging U.S. Human Rights Violations Since 9/11*. Having been a prisoner before, I can only imagine what goes on at Guantanamo Bay. And speculate on the songs, chants, prayers and poetry that might come from there in the near future.

Nevertheless it is beyond dispute in the West today that some sections of the media and lovers of freedom throughout the world are concerned about the erosion of civil liberties and human rights ushered in after 9/11, where the arbitrary arrests of presumed terrorists, the locking up of merely suspected terrorists and the terrifying legislation that is coming into play, have become or are in danger of becoming the norm.

And in Britain after the 7/7 attacks in 2005, the story of how one suspected terrorist was gunned down on the London Underground threatens to be told endlessly; other suspected terrorists are still being severely dealt with by the authorities. Furthermore, in order to deter potential terrorists the UK Government has been forced to introduce unsettling legislation. Desperate measures to increase the number of prisons and establish projects like ASBOs, anti-social behaviour orders, which purport to protect the ordinary citizens from local thugs, have come to the fore. Clearly, we need to develop a balanced mindset in order to appreciate the problems that confront us in the prisonised communities where we live. And critically studying Literatures of Incarceration texts might be one of the many ways of beginning to understand a world which is in danger of creating unacceptable gulags of the twenty-first century.

Obviously the arbitrariness of arrests of presumed terrorists and their transfer to secret locations across the globe, appearing on the scene long after the fall of the Berlin Wall, the end of the Cold War with its concomitant Communism, and the official abolition of apartheid in South Africa, is embarrassing to everyone who loves freedom. More so because most of the security grounds that are invoked for the justification of these random arrests and detentions defy logic in a world where even the notion of 'terrorist' itself has become so nebulous, so fuzzy, so ill-defined or not even defined at all, that it makes a mockery of the authorities who apply it to their given individuals in society.

Strategies for surviving prisons

It is undeniable that Literatures of Incarceration texts can inspire readers and perhaps cause them to appreciate the nature of the prison in which we live, to translate William Shakespeare's Richard II.[7] From the texts, we learn that the prisons where we live are varied, often with fascinating origins. For example, during their colonial rule of Africa, European countries transferred their prisons to the African continent in curious ways. When the British arrested Kwame Nkrumah of Ghana, Kenneth Kaunda of Zambia and Josiah Mwangi Kariuki of Kenya, to name only three who were once presumed to have been the most 'notorious' terrorists, they dumped them into prisons that were in effect African bushes infested by snakes and wild animals. Then they went on to fabricate the lies that the so-called nationalists were in fact cannibals who would eat the children of the people among whom they had been dumped.[8]

In the struggle for the liberation of their countries from European colonialists, therefore, such African nationalists were forced to fight on two fronts. They had to justify their cause to the European powers who illegally occupied their land as well as try to convince the people among whom they were dumped that they were liberators of the territories that Europeans occupied, and not the cannibals that the colonisers claimed they were. As for the transfer of prisoners, when Hastings Banda and his staunch supporters fought the British to give Nyasaland Protectorate independence, British soldiers and police rounded them up at dawn – Banda himself still in his pyjamas – and flew them into Southern Rhodesia where they were dumped in HM prisons Gweru, Khami and others – there some stayed for about two years.

And whoever turned Robben Island into the ultimate prison for the so-called 'notorious terrorists' like Nelson Mandela in apartheid South Africa must have learnt the trick of isolating political leaders from their supporters and transferring them from one prison to another or from one part of the country to another, which had been prevalent in the USSR, in Germany under Hitler and throughout Europe. There is nothing strange, then, about the choice of Guantanamo Bay and the transfer of presumed terrorists there by the US government; there is nothing strange about the establishment of detention centres in Europe, including those not far from Oxford and throughout the UK. Although we like to forget the point, for many years such prisons have become an integral part of Western civilisation.

But I insist. The world is replete with subtly crafted memoirs and testimonies on incarceration, which can be fruitfully studied as literature in its own right. For many years writers have written novels, essays, poetry and plays about their imprisonment, their fight for justice and their struggle to restore the dignity they or others have lost. A careful study of these texts might help us to develop an appropriate mindset and tools for the treatment of our 'prisonised' societies. Of course, we can understand the history of European prisons by reading texts such as Michel Foucault's *Discipline and Punish: The Birth of the Prison*.[9] But transfers of presumed terrorists, rebels, dissidents, nationalists and others from one part of the globe to another, and the complex concerns dogged by our prisonised world, are depicted more imaginatively in some texts on Literatures of Incarceration. This is why reading such literature might help us redress our sometimes untenable positions on who are terrorists and who are patriots, and who are not. This is how we might gain a balanced knowledge of the prisons or bushes in which we live. After all, might the true prison be 'not the leaking roof / Nor the singing mosquitoes / In the damp, wretched cell', but within us, as the executed Nigerian writer and publisher Ken Saro-Wiwa once declared?[10]

The relevance of Literatures of Incarceration

The subject matter of Literatures of Incarceration is depressing, even horrific – that we cannot deny; and in many ways it is this aspect that challenges the concept of 'enjoyment', which we are supposed to get from engaging in such creative texts. But as I have intimated, most writers craft their incarceration so imaginatively and with such humour, albeit bleak, that the end product, I dare to suggest, compares favourably with the great tragedies of our times. The relevance to our modern world of the subject matter of Literatures of Incarceration as serious literature should therefore not be a contentious issue.

Take a few instances. In one of the most readable little novels, *Night*, Elie Wiesel brilliantly depicts the trains that transported Jews to gas chambers during the Holocaust and, for those who survived the journey, the horrific lives they lived there, often without hope and without God.[11] Alexander Solzhenitsyn's novels such as *The First Circle* and *One Day in the Life of Ivan Denisovich*, or his play *Prisoners* and other works, vividly portray the arbitrary arrests suffered by presumed Russian political dissidents, their transportation to labour camps in Siberia and their struggle for survival in extremely cold and inhuman environments, often against the greatest odds imaginable.[12]

In *The Resistance Trilogy* the Chilean writer Ariel Dorfman turns into powerful drama three critical areas that confront governments and particularly dictatorships today. *Widows* is a play about the women who wait vacantly for their fathers, husbands, brothers and male children who have been 'disappeared' under General Augusto Pinochet's dictatorship in Chile. *Reader* depicts how censorship can be self-inflicting and self-destructive in such dictatorships, but the issues that the text raises are similar to those that worry us about the kind of legislation that curtails freedoms after 9/11 and 7/7. *Death and the Maiden* tackles the vexing questions surrounding the notion of reconciliation with torturers: one victim of rape meets the man who raped her, and pertinent moral and other questions on what constitutes true reconciliation are subtly negotiated.[13]

Nawal El Saadawi's *Memoirs from the Women's Prison* is a moving account of resistance to state violence on women, which compares favourably with the depiction of the struggle against state brutality on women in *Grey is the Colour of Hope* by the poet and novelist Irina Ratushinskaya. This in turn compares and contrasts with the classical Russian prison writings by Anna Akhmatova, Osip Mandelstam, Nikolai Zabolotsky and others, or Oscar Wilde's *The Ballad of Reading Gaol*; or for that matter John Bunyan's *Pilgrim's Progress* or, even further back, the Bible. And then there are extracts from prison memoirs like *Wall Tappings*, an anthology edited by Judith Scheffler; there are other texts that will take their natural place in the critical study of the Literatures of Incarceration that one envisages.[14]

The politics of denial

Today after 9/11 and 7/7 reports and stories of the transfer of presumed terrorists, often at night, to secret locations across the globe for their detention, interrogation, to be tortured and even to be 'disappeared', meet robust denials. But such denials did not start in the twenty-first century; they did not start with the experience of Abu Ghraib or Guantanamo Bay; they did not start with the struggle of asylum seekers in British, French and other European detention centres. The Nazis denied the Holocaust with as much vigour and often in boastful language too. In *The Drowned and the Saved*, Primo Levi quotes the following SS boast from Simon Wiesenthal's book, *The Murderers Are Among Us*:

> However this war may end, we have won the war against you; none of you will be left to bear witness, but even if someone were to survive, the world would not believe him. There will perhaps be suspicions, discussions, research by historians, but there will be no certainties, because we will destroy the evidence together with you. And even if some proof should remain and some of you survive, people will say that the events you describe are the exaggerations of Allied propaganda and will believe us, who will deny everything, and not you. We will be the ones to dictate the history of the Lagers.[15]

Three years ago the Edinburgh branch of Amnesty International asked me to send a postcard to journalist and writer U Win Tin, who was imprisoned indefinitely for belonging to Aung San Suu Kyi's pro-democracy opposition party in Burma. In March 2005 U Win Tin was celebrating his seventy-fifth birthday still in Insein prison in Burma. My Edinburgh friend suggested that the Burmese Amnesty International's prisoner of conscience seemed to be in danger of being another victim of protest fatigue. I offered the following effort to satirise his jailors' boastful denial of his existence.

On U Win Tin's 75th Birthday (March, 2005)[16]
'U Win Tin, on this your seventy-fifth
birthday, we your jailors have the pleasure
to remind you that you are still being
held under Emergency Provisions Acts
bequeathed by the British. You are
still being accused of thinking, speaking
out, feeling and inciting others so to do.
You'll continue to be incarcerated for
promoting what you call freedom of speech
and we call sheltering traitors or those
likely so to be. We'll still condemn you
to sleep on cold concrete floors without
blankets or mats, alone or with others
in cells three paces by two. And should
you think, feel, speak out about these
or similar matters, we'll dump you in
solitary confinement cells again whether

your rotting teeth grind, your aching back
throbs or your eyesight begins to die. And
Should you,
on this your seventy-fifth birthday, need
family for medication, food, warmth, we've
been directed by the powers that be to let
you have monthly family visits. Should
you try to smuggle out notes to your UN
friends and others outside these Burmese
islands, should we find, God forbid, after
our strip searches, you possess proscribed
effects like little radio sets, magazines, pens,
newspaper cuttings from overseas human
rights campaigns for your release, expect
thunderous crack down to strike you like
lightning. And should you attempt to smile,
laugh, sing, break wind, even accidentally,
to celebrate this your seventy-fifth birthday,
we your jailors will show you what bars
Insein Prison is capable of imposing on
fragile bones like yours. For you, U Win
Tin, are a shameless dissident, and another
notorious terrorist to their excellencies up
on high. And the war we are waging against
characters like you is total and we intend
to win, we swear by our security reasons!
So, there you have it, your position again
perfectly clarified, how do you plead now?'

The point that needs stressing is that wherever they have had the opportunity, the survivors of incarceration, the Holocaust, the gulag, or dictatorships in Latin America, Africa, China or Asia, have provided their own counter-boasts to confront the authorities who tortured them. And the challenge has often taken the form of Russia's foremost master of creative incarceration, Osip Mandelstam, who once taunted his torturers with the reminder that 'You left me my lips, and they shape words, even in silence.'[17]

'Never drop your guard'

Let me conclude by reiterating my position on creative incarceration and the strategies for surviving freedom. If you should ever be incarcerated without trial and without charge (imagine another victim of Guantanamo Bay); if you should be lucky enough to have a prayerful family, dedicated friends, colleagues and compatriots as well as strangers who can influence distinguished writers, linguists, churchmen and churchwomen, journalists, broadcasters, politicians, Amnesty International, Pen International, Africa Watch, Human Rights Watch and other human rights activists and groups, to fight for your freedom; if you should then be liberated, say after three years, seven months, sixteen days and more than twelve hours and end up in exile, say in Britain; consider yourself fortunate: the first battle has been won, but the war for surviving your freedom has only just begun.

Your prison was not easy. You survived their poisonous food, enduring fortnightly bouts of malaria, cholera and diarrhoea, because God provided the antidote; you cheered yourselves up by telling one another stories of your lives, often repeating them many times over until your teeth turned black; then you told one another downright lies, adding this and that to old repertoires, until the plots thickened beyond recognition and the distinction between fact and fiction vanished. And without being allowed family visits for twenty-two months, you desperately though surreptitiously sent notes to family and friends until your Lifebuoy and Sunlight soap wrappers and the toilet paper you used ran out. You began to compose poems in your head, narrative spirals of poems that you hoped your memory would spew out if and when you were finally liberated.

But do not be alarmed when you can only recover twenty of the twenty-five titles of the poems your memory could hold. And remember, as you did your time in prison, the world did not stand still for you, it never does, however innocent you might be. And in your case remember you have so much to catch up on: the Gulf War has been and gone, the Berlin Wall has crumbled and with it the Cold War and Iron Curtain, and in South Africa Nelson Mandela has been released and the notorious social, cultural, political system of apartheid officially abolished – you have a whole brave new world out there to confront.

Alone you played pragmatic games on the relevance-theoretic interpretation of Biblical riddles and parables and sometimes smiled at the futility both of the exercise and of life. But after gazing at the blank walls of your stinking cells for so long, do not count on your theoretical linguistics for possible employment; the subject might have moved beyond recognition on your release. Do not bank on teaching Commonwealth literature either; while you were put away that discipline has been renamed postcolonial literature, and a popular critical framework for its analysis called postcolonial theory has evolved. Now, most scholars who are engaged in cultural studies are happily cashing in on the new theory, each assuming its relevance in their respective discipline. That kind of academic world is scary; therefore, prepare to reinvent yourself in other ways. Begin reading and re-reading African and other prison writings: poetry, plays, testimonies, diaries, journals and memoirs. You will rediscover how imprisoned writers have survived their incarceration and their liberation throughout the years; and perhaps you will pinch one or two tricks from those predecessors you revere, to enable you to craft your own memoir later.

And do not forget that after three years, seven months, sixteen days and more than twelve hours of crushing mosquitoes and scorpions at night; and despite the three Bibles for your only library that you shared with ninety other prisoners; you did your time without radio, newspaper or police magazine stories to entertain you. Concede, therefore, that you might have to learn again how to read; admit that you find it difficult to complete reading even your favourite novel, *Pride and Prejudice*, which in better times you read once a year; and acknowledge that even flicking through the pages of the *TLS* and the *Guardian*, which was your favourite pursuit when you were a student at University College London once, has become cumbersome after about four years of gazing at blank walls.

But do not despair. Remember the strategies that Irina Ratushinskaya depicted in her *Grey is the Colour of Hope*. For, with her fellow cellmates, the Russian poet and novelist decided to survive willy-nilly; they went on hunger strikes, fought and quarrelled with prison guards and among themselves; they prayed tediously for release and for the safety of their families; they were often on the brink of despairing even of God. Ratushinskaya herself had been writing poems on torn sheets of the Bible, toilet paper and other unlikely places and sending these secretly to the outside world for translation and publication.

All the while the poet and her cellmates had no clue as to the extent of the campaign for their release that was being mounted by Amnesty International, Pen International, Human Rights Watch and other human rights organisations, and eminent writers, friends and strangers around the globe. She realised only after her liberation that it was this global campaign that had forced President Reagan of the US and President Gorbachev of the USSR to review her case at their meeting in Reykjavik. So, if you should ever want to make time out of the chaos of your liberation and exile (imagine another Guantanamo Bay victim released), find the stamina to rethink your spatial, temporal and narrative spirals, in order to survive your freedom.

Above all, do not forget the quintessential strategy for the creative incarceration that led to the liberation of the imprisoned poet and her cellmates, as clearly set out at the beginning of *Grey is the Colour of Hope*:

> So here I am, riding along in a black Volga. They said that they are taking me home. For Good. A 'clean' release. They have even returned my passport without any entry about my criminal record. And to cap it all, they even offered generously to drive me home – in a KGB car. What can all this mean? I sit in the car, trying to gather my wits. They are watching me, so I must not show any sign of confusion, any emotion at all. The reflexes evolved during four years of imprisonment function automatically – never trust them! Never drop your guard![18]

Notes

1 First appeared in Jack Mapanje, *Skipping Without Ropes* (Newcastle upon Tyne: Bloodaxe Books, 1998).

2 Peter Benenson, 'The forgotten prisoners' *Observer* (28 May 1961) Weekend Review section, p. 1.
3 Angela Y. Davis, *Abolition Democracy: Beyond Prisons, Torture and Empire* (New York: Seven Stories Press, 2005).
4 Ann Fagan Ginger, *Challenging U.S. Human Rights Violations Since 9/11* (Amhurst, NY: Prometheus Books, 2005).
5 *Ibid.*, p. 138.
6 *Ibid.*, p. 137.
7 'I have been studying how I may compare / This prison where I live unto the world: / And for because the world is populous, / And here is not a creature but myself, / I cannot do it; yet I'll hammer it out.' W. Shakespeare, *Richard II*, Act V, scene 5.
8 See Jack Mapanje (ed.), *Gathering Seaweed: African Prison Writing* (Oxford: Heinemann African Writers Series, 2002).
9 M. Foucault, *Discipline and Punish: The Birth of the Prison* (London: Allen Lane, 1977).
10 'The True Prison', from Ken Saro-Wiwa, *A Month and a Day: A Detention Diary* (London: Penguin, 1995).
11 Elie Wiesel, *Night* (London: MacGibbon and Kee, 1960).
12 A. Solzhenitsyn, *The First Circle* (London: Collins and Harville Press, 1968); *One Day in the Life of Ivan Denisovich* (London: Gollancz, 1965); *Prisoners* (London: Bodley Head, 1983).
13 A. Dorfman, *The Resistance Trilogy* (London: Nick Hearn, 1998; originally published: *Widows*: 1983; *Death and the Maiden*: 1991; *Reader*: 1995).
14 N. el Saadawi, *Memoirs from the Women's Prison* (London: Women's Press, 1986); I. Ratushinskaya, *Grey is the Colour of Hope* (London: Hodder and Stoughton, 1988); O. Wilde, *The Ballad of Reading Gaol* (London: Phoenix, 1996, originally 1898); J. Bunyan, *The Pilgrim's Progress* (Oxford: Oxford University Press, 2003, originally 1678); Judith A. Scheffler (ed.), *Wall Tappings: An International Anthology of Women's Prison Writings 200 to the Present* (New York: Feminist Press at the City University of New York, 2002).
15 P. Levi, *The Drowned and the Saved* (London: Vintage, 1989).
16 First published in *Beasts of Nalunga* (Tarset, Northumberland: Bloodaxe Books, 2007).
17 Untitled poems number 307, *The Selected Poems of Osip Mandelstam*, translated C. Brown and W. S. Merwin (London: Oxford University Press, 1973).
18 I. Ratushinskaya, *Grey is the Colour of Hope*, as in note 14, p. 5.

6a Jonny Steinberg

'With no amulet to protect him': a South African response to Jack Mapanje

There is a story about Nelson Mandela, one that his biographers skate over hastily and without enthusiasm, for it has about it an air of awkwardness.

Shortly after his release from prison in 1990, Mandela commissioned a house to be built for himself in Qunu, the Transkei village of his childhood. He envisaged vacationing there from time to time, to be sure, but what he had his eye on principally was a place in which to live out his retirement. Aside from being South Africa's prospective president, he was also seventy-one years old, an age at which one thinks about these things.

The architect commissioned to design the house was given the most unusual brief. He was to approach the Department of Prisons, Mandela instructed, and acquire the architectural plans of a cottage situated in the grounds of Viktor Verster prison in Paarl. He was to copy that cottage precisely, from the size and shape of each room to the colour of the brick-faced exterior. The new house, he was told, must be exactly like the one in the prison grounds. The cottage in question housed Nelson Mandela during the last two years of his twenty-seven-year incarceration. The desire which he was instructing his architect to give expression to was to spend his retirement living in a replica of his place of confinement. A nervous journalist asked Mandela in the mid-1990s what was going through his mind when he made this decision. He chortled in the warm and grandfatherly way for which he was now famous, and then brushed the question aside with some flippancy: he wanted a place, he said, where he could find the kitchen in the middle of the night without banging his shins.

The source of this story's awkwardness is quite simple. Of all the human beings who have served lengthy prison terms, Mandela is surely the one we would least want to hanker after the cocoon of his erstwhile cell. His release, after all, was a moment of clean and massive redemption, both for him personally, and for an entire nation. Indeed, the triumph belonged not just to South Africa, but to humanity as a whole; as Mandela left Viktor Verster behind him, so our species left behind it the last statutory trace of white supremacy. One does not want such a man to choose a replica of his jail in which to retire and to die. For if the story of his freedom is indeed ours, what does the fact that prison clings to *him*, of all former prisoners, tell us about ourselves?

Jack Mapanje's release from a Malawian jail in 1991 was incomparable to Mandela's in so many ways. Mandela's home country embraced him as a living god. Mapanje's exiled him. Mandela became president of a fêted liberation movement and then of South Africa. Mapanje arrived on Britain's shores penniless and unemployed, and the head of a household of five. If Mandela's relation to his past as an incarcerated man turned out to be more complicated than expected, can one imagine Mapanje's?

Mapanje came to the United Kingdom as an involuntary exile and as a black African immigrant in search of a livelihood. Like all immigrants, he had to peddle his wares; he had to show his hosts what he had to offer. The problem, Mapanje complains, is that his three and a half years in Hastings Banda's prison cells had ruined his craft. 'My imprisonment gave me no opportunity', he says wryly, 'to blossom as a linguist.' He thought briefly of trying his hand at literary scholarship, but found the field in which he was interested, Third World literature, to be dominated by postcolonial studies, a genre of scholarship buried under an abstruse and laborious language for which he held little affection.

But the problem lay deeper than that; Mapanje felt that he had lost his grip on more than just his craft. The Berlin Wall had fallen during his incarceration, the Cold War had ended, apartheid was dying. The world was changing very fast, and Mapanje felt not only that it had left him behind, but that he had lost the capacity to catch up. 'After four academic years of not being allowed a pen, paper, newspapers or radio', he tells us, 'and with only three Bibles to be shared among ninety political and condemned prisoners for our library – after gazing at filthy prison walls for so long – I had almost forgotten how to read.'

Under the burden of having to support a family and make a new life in a foreign country, Mapanje began to reinvent himself. His back against the wall, he turned his ordeal into something he might sell. Rather than as a man ruined by prison, he presented himself to the academy as a scholar whose incarceration had given him insight. In writing of his own experience of jail and its aftermath, and in teaching the writings of others who had been imprisoned, he could bring some-thing new to the study and the teaching of literature, something valuable enough to be exchanged for a post at a university, for a salary. He peddled this idea shyly at first, without much hope of success. And the returns he reaped were indeed for a long time very meagre. But with his persistence, and with the gathering appreciation for the obvious value of what he was providing, came success. Hence the Oxford Amnesty Lecture to which this is a response: an essay by a man who, after a long and uncertain battle, has made of a potentially ruinous experience a vocation and a career.

As stories of incarceration and its aftermath go, this is a very warming one. To pluck from so grim and subtractive an ordeal both a livelihood and a rich vein of intellectual work tells a tale, like Mandela's, of redemption.

But I suspect that there may be another side to Mapanje's story, an underside, perhaps. Mapanje talks at length of the hardships he experienced when he came to the UK, but what he does not speak of is how it felt to carry his awful prison experience around with him and to peddle it to one academic institution after another. Was it humiliating? How did it feel, as a black African, to knock on the doors of office upon office with this terrible episode in his briefcase, to pitch it as a sales-man pitches his wares? Were there not times when he wished he could move beyond those three and a half years and retrieve the tools of the craft he practised before the nightmare began? Perhaps he does not mention these things because he did not feel them, but I wonder whether there were not times when he felt he was eternally chained to those three and a half years.

Mandela fashioned the place of his incarceration into the home he imagined would shelter him in his old age. Mapanje used his as a tool to attain the means to have a house at all. Both stories are happy ones, but neither is uncomplicated.

Let me explain the angle from which I come to Mapanje's story. My experience of prisons is as a researcher of South Africa's century-old prison gangs. The inmates I have gotten to know well thus have little in common with Jack Mapanje. Among them are rapists, murderers, thieves; all are men who run grim and violent inmate regimes behind the bars of South Africa's jails.

And yet when I began reading Jack Mapanje's words I felt pinpricks of recognition all over my body. The story he tells is so utterly similar to the one I have heard from the lips of scores of criminals when they describe how it feels to return to the outside world after a long period inside. The corrosiveness of those missing years, the shocking discovery that they have nibbled away at one's capacity to read, to think, to concentrate for more than a few moments at a time; the horrifying thought that one has been stripped of one's competence and may never be able to function in the outside world again. Mapanje's is of course a special case: not every prisoner loses his country and his profession; not every prisoner was jailed because he did right rather than wrong. Nonetheless, what struck me as I read his essay was its familiarity.

I recalled in particular a spectacle I had witnessed in the central courtyard at Pollsmoor prison in Cape Town in 2002. It was a highly unusual day in the prison's life: South Africa's Minister of Correctional Services was there to address prisoners and staff; several hundred inmates sat in long rows in their bright orange overalls listening very politely to what the Minister had to say. When he was done, the master of ceremonies took questions from the floor. The first inmate who rose to speak was a 59-year-old prison veteran called Solomon Moses. He was positively ancient by inmate standards, 'a man in the clouds', in prison language. I had seen him often on the inside, a quiet, detached man shuffling down the prison corridors on stiff legs.

Now, as he began addressing the Minister, he spoke with a force I had not imagined he possessed.

'I am due to leave these walls in less than a month from now', he began. 'A month from today, I will be in the world outside. I will see everything – the streets, the cars, the shops – as if I am a free man. And yet between me and this world there will be an invisible wall, a glass wall. I will be able to see the world, but not touch it. I will be able to smell it, but not be a part of it. Mark my words, it will not be long before I am back behind these walls. That is my fate.'

A few seconds into Moses' talk, quiet murmurs of affirmation rose from the inmate audience. By the time he mentioned invisible walls the murmurs had become shouts. And when he declared that it was his fate to return, every inmate leapt from his seat and roared and shouted and whistled, the courtyard now a din of strange and unpredictable energy. The master of ceremonies and the Minister glanced at one another nervously.

South Africa's prison gangs, to which Moses and most of the prisoners in that courtyard belonged, are grounded in an extraordinary oral history, a kind of creation myth, one that has been passed by word of mouth from one generation of prisoners to the next since the first decade of the twentieth century. It tells the mythologised story of a real historical figure who walked the streets of early Johannesburg, a bandit leader and a rogue called Nongoloza Mathebula. The story South African prisoners have been telling about Nongoloza over the last century has many layers. In part it is a justification for crime as anti-colonial banditry. In part it is an explanation of homoerotic relations behind bars. But the most important aspect of the tale for my purposes here is the eerie comfort it gives to men who find themselves in Solomon Moses' position, men who are about to walk into the outside world and know that they will not cope there.

'Where you are going now', the prison gang incantation tells newly recruited members, 'you will not be seeing your mother or your father. They are behind you now, and you cannot retrace your steps. And so you no longer have a mother. You no longer have a father. Nongoloza is your father now. He will be your father until you die.'

This story functions as a kind of a charm or amulet; it takes a prisoner's deepest fear, that when he returns to the world he will no longer be able to function there, and turns it into a virtue. 'Don't worry', the prison gang incantation tells him. 'You now have us. You can always come back.' A version of the same ritual was re-enacted that day in the Pollsmoor courtyard when the Minister came to speak. Solomon Moses announced that the world outside was lost to him; that's fine, the roars and whistles of the crowd replied: you can come back to us.

I believe that every prison culture anywhere in the world fabricates such an amulet. The fear Jack Mapanje remembers feeling when he came to the United Kingdom, that the world had moved on and that he would never catch up, that he had indeed been stripped of the means to catch up, is a universal prisoner's fear. What makes Mapanje's story a radical one is that he had no amulet to protect him from this fate. South African prison gangsters carry the eternal promise of being able to return to Nongoloza. Nelson Mandela could imagine his refuge from the world as the place of his confinement, and he had the means to build a real house from this fantasy. Mapanje had neither of these options. Prison clung to him as it clings to all former prisoners. He was forced to make this burden light, not heavy; he had to go out into the world with his prison experience hanging round his neck and he knew that he must either sink or swim.

And so the road to the position Mapanje now occupies as a teacher, a writer and a poet is both familiar and unusual. It is an eccentric variation of a universal post-imprisonment story. His essay takes its place among the literatures of incarceration next to the tale gangsters tell of Nongoloza, and the story Mandela tells of the steps he took to avoid bashing his shins in the night.

Index